PRACTICAL
WATERCOLOR
TECHNIQUES

EDITED BY SARAH BUCKLEY

Crescent Books
New York/Avenel, New Jersey

A QUINTET BOOK

This 1992 edition published by
Crescent Books, distributed by
Outlet Books Company Inc.
a Random House Company
40 Engelhard Avenue, Avenel, New Jersey 07001

ISBN 0-517-07015-4

8 7 6 5 4 3 2 1

This book was designed and produced by
Quintet Publishing Limited
6 Blundell Street
London N7 9BH

Designer: Mike Spiller
Editor: Sarah Buckley

Typeset in Great Britain by
En to En Typesetters, Tunbridge Wells
Manufactured in Singapore by
Chroma Graphics (Overseas) PTE. LTD.
Printed in Spain by
Graficas Estella, S.A. Navarra.

The material in this publication previously
appeared in other books.

·CONTENTS·

• CHAPTER ONE •

Materials and Equipment

A BRIEF HISTORY

Transparency and the soft harmony of color washes, with highlights and lighter areas rendered by leaving the white paper bare or faintly toned, are the main characteristics of "pure" watercolor painting.

The color cannot be worked on its ground to the same extent as with oils or other opaque media — errors cannot be merely painted over, for instance — so that a higher standard of technique may be required to produce a satisfactory watercolor painting. But the freshness and brilliance of a good watercolor are ample compensation for the time spent in acquiring sound technique.

Since the time of the ancient Egyptians, water has been used as a diluent in many types of paint, including size paint, distemper, fresco, tempera, and gouache. True watercolor, however, consists solely of very finely ground pigment with gum arabic (known sometimes as gum senegal) as the binder.

The water-soluble gum acts as a light varnish, giving the colors a greater brightness and sheen.

Other substances, including sugar syrup and glycerin, may occasionally be added to the water in making up the paint. The syrup acts as a plasticizer, making the painting smoother; and the glycerin is said to lend extra brilliance, and in warm weather prevents the paint from drying too quickly.

White pigment is never used in a pure watercolor palette. Its addition creates, in effect, a different medium — gouache, and this book includes some advice about this medium.

Although many medieval illustrators used pure — that is transparent — watercolor in small works and on manuscripts, others added opaque or body color to make a background on which gold leaf was laid. The first European fully to recognize the value of the medium in larger works, using it extensively in landscape paintings, was the German artist Albrecht Dürer (1471-1528). Although strong lines and opaque passages played their part, the unique transparency of watercolor washes was a major feature of these works.

One of the earliest English artists to make full and effective use of the medium was John White, a draftsman with Sir Walter Raleigh's 1585 expedition to the coast of North America. White's use of the full range of watercolor in clean washes, when making drawings for the record of the life and scenery of the North Carolina coast, have caused some historians to claim him as the "father" of the English watercolor school.

Indeed, on the Continent, watercolor became known as "the English art"; but it was not until nearly two centuries later, in the latter part of the eighteenth century, that the art blossomed into its full pride and distinction in the hands of such painters as Paul Sandby (1725-1809), William Blake (1757-1827), Thomas Girtin (1755-1802), J.M.W. Turner (1755-1851), John Crome (1763-1821), John Sell Cotman (1782-1842), John Varley (1788-1842), David Cox (1783-1859), and Peter de Wint (1784–1849).

Only those who have mastered a basic technique and recognized the limitations of a medium can afford to depart from the rules and, in doing so, evolve new styles. Thomas Girtin, for example, regarded the limitations of watercolor as a challenge and, in effect, increased the challenge by deliberately restricting the range of his palette. He used only five basic colors: yellow ocher, burnt sienna, light red, monastral blue, and ivory black. He applied the paint in thin washes, allowing each wash to dry before applying the next, building up deep tonal gradations and contrasts. Like most of the "English school," he left areas of white paper untouched to provide highlights, but occasionally broke a "rule" by using gouache for a highlight.

William Blake devised something akin to offset printing to apply his first layers of color, painting on an impervious surface such as glass, porcelain, or glazed stiff paper, and pressing this over his painting paper. When the "print" was dry he worked over it in opaque or body color to elaborate and enliven it.

J.M.W. Turner virtually forced the paint to obey his rules, shifting it while wet, scumbling, and scratching it on heavy paper until gleaming and glowing effects were produced — unrecognizable at first as true watercolor. He mixed techniques and made them compatible. In *Tintern Abbey* he built up strong tonal contrasts with flat and broken washes. Heavy wet-into-wet methods, scumbles, and dry-brush strokes were all combined in the harmonies of *Kilgarran Castle*; while *Venice from the Giudecca* is alive with thin, wet washes and delicate touches of opaque paint.

Tne Victorian age saw a rise in the general popularity of watercolor painting, particularly in Britain; and some Victorian artists, including

John Everett Millais (1829-1896), found a ready sale for watercolor copies of their larger oil paintings. Watercolor had already been used for the opposite process – making quick color sketches for later rendering as larger works in oil – by such masters as van Dyck (1599-1641), Gainsborough (1727-1788), and Constable (1776-1837).

They discovered that quick-drying watercolor enabled them to experiment with color contrasts and make swift notes of passing atmospheric effects, such as mists, rainbows, changing reflections, and fast-altering cloud formations.

America's tradition of watercolor painting, although not so long as that of England, is soundly based on the work of fine exponents like Winslow Homer (1830-1910), who did much for the art in the States (although appreciation was slow to come: fine paintings of his were selling for as little as 75 dollars in 1880). The tradition was carried on by Thomas Eakins (1844-1916), Edward Hopper (1882-1967), and Andrew Wyeth (born 1917). Ben Shahn (1898-1969) used the medium with great fluidity, especially in the expression of social ideas, exemplified by his *Martin Luther King*, painted in 1966.

The English tradition has been carried on strongly by such major artists as Edward Burra (1905-1976), Paul Nash (1889-1946), and David Jones (born 1895). On the Continent, Paul Klee (1879-1940), a founder member of the Bauhaus, used watercolor for some of his most significant work. His *Motif of Mammamet* shows a striking use of colors contrasted in small, rough-edged, carefully-proportioned washes which reveal the texture of the paper beneath.

The distinction between fine art and the art of the illustrator, always blurred, became more so in the nineteenth century, with the invention of half-tone reproduction. Overlaying of red, yellow, and blue inks, broken down by screens to produce many tones, made possible the reproduction of illustrations in full color. Watercolor was found to be an ideal medium to submit to the process, which enabled books containing full-color illustrations to be produced comparatively cheaply for the mass market. Among the many fine artists who used watercolor for their illustration originals are Arthur Rackham (1867-1939) and Edmund Dulac (1882-1953). Dulac outlined and pointed up many of his drawings with India ink. In printing – although the black itself could not be reproduced by the three-color process – this tended to soften and enhance the watercolor washes lying within his outlines.

SUPPORTS

The most widely-used watercolor support is paper, which is manufactured for the purpose in a wide variety of weights and textures.

Ignoring the many cheap papers made up into children's "drawing and painting books," there are three main categories of real watercolor paper: hot-pressed or HP; cold-pressed (CP) – which is also known as "not" paper in Britain ("not" for "not-pressed"); and rough.

Hot-pressed is very smooth, and suitable for line and wash. Many artists find it too slippery for pure watercolor work. Cold-pressed is the most popular all-round paper. Its semi-rough surface takes large, even washes very well, but a quickly-dragged dryish brush will also bring up what roughness it possesses, so that smooth and rough surfaces are obtainable on the same sheet. Fine detail can also be rendered on cold-pressed paper.

Rough paper has a definite "tooth" to it. It drags at the brush. This produces a speckled effect, with pigment settling in the lower parts of the surface, leaving the rest white. This is fine for rendering, say, the sparkle of sunshine on water; but the overall appearance of the picture is inclined to be monotonous in the hands of a beginner if he or she cannot achieve, as contrast, the deep, even, wet washes which the expert can produce on the roughest paper.

Hand-made papers are of the highest quality – and the most expensive. They are mainly of pure linen rag, bleached without chemicals, or with chemicals that are thoroughly neutralized; and they are sized on one side only. This correct painting side faces the artist when the paper, held up to the light, shows the maker's water-mark the right way around.

Japanese rice papers, fragile and absorbent, are obtainable in the United States and Europe; and some Western artists have experimented with them successfully for delicate work. Among the brands available are Kozo, Mitsumata and Gambi. Kozo is the strongest.

Tinted papers are sometimes used, especially for reproduction work; but the basic tint may not be as permanent as the colors laid on it, and its change could affect the overall tone of the picture in time. Many artists prefer to apply their own tint with thin wash and a sponge.

Good handmade or machine made papers for watercolor painting will have a clearly visible watermark (◄). The right side of the paper to work on is the side on which the watermark can be seen the right way round. Three main surfaces are available (►) hot-pressed, a fairly smooth surface, not (or cold pressed) paper, which is semi-rough, and rough.

The weight or thickness of a watercolor paper is as important a consideration as its surface. Weight is measured by the ream. A 70lb paper, for instance, means that 480 sheets of it – a ream – weighs 70lb.

Light papers may need stretching to prevent them from buckling under heavy washes. Heavier papers, of 140lb and upward, can be clipped to a board and used for direct work.

In general, the weight of the paper, and its price, increases in proportion to the size of the ready-cut sheets, so that an artist who wishes to use a heavier paper in a smaller size may have to cut it from a larger sheet. However, the medium and most popular size, 30 × 22in (75 × 55cm), has the greatest range of weights associated with it: from 70lb to 300lb.

Names associated with good artists' papers include the Strathmore Paper Company, Saunders, R.W.S. (Royal Watercolour Society), Bockingford, Crisbrook, d'Arches, Arnold, Green, Fabriano, Michallet, and Ingres. Hand-made papers include the 90lb R.W.S., Saunders and tinted Fabriano paper.

A good paper for beginners in the medium is Saunders machine-made 90lb, 30 × 22in, with cold-pressed surface. It is tough, stretches well if needed to take heavy washes, and stands up well to drawing and erasing.

All watercolor papers should be stored in as dry a place as possible. Damp may activate chemical impurities, producing spots which will not take color.

A number of manufacturers produce excellent papers for watercolor work. A number of different examples are shown (▼). When a paper is selected, the weight, texture, and tone required must be carefully considered. It may be preferable to use white paper and, if a tint is required, apply a wash paint all over to achieve the right color, but a good range of tinted papers is available. The texture should be chosen according to how much white will be seen through the paint. A smooth paper will rapidly become covered with color, but the heavily textured papers leave tiny white flecks showing through a watercolor wash.

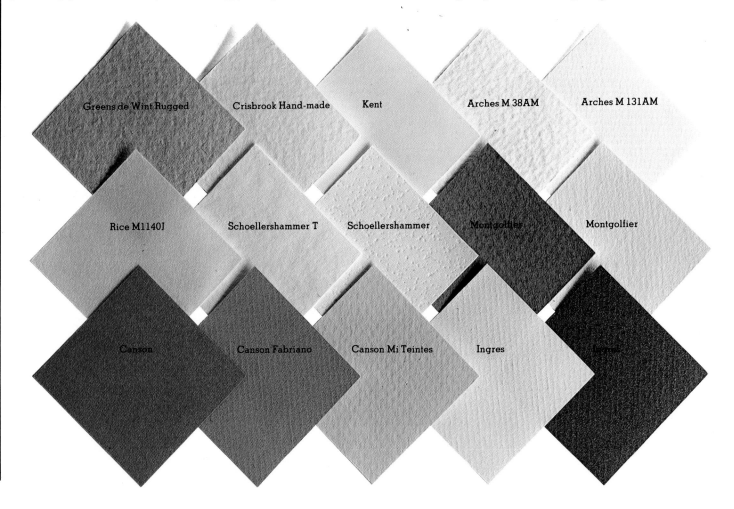

Greens de Wint Rugged · Crisbrook Hand-made · Kent · Arches M 38AM · Arches M 131AM · Rice M1140J · Schoellershammer T · Schoellershammer · Montgolfier · Montgolfier · Canson · Canson Fabriano · Canson Mi Teintes · Ingres

STRETCHING PAPER

Lightweight papers, which tend to buckle when washes are applied, should be stretched before use. There are a number of different methods.

The simplest, for studio use, is to wet the paper thoroughly by laying it in a tray of water. Holding it by the edge, shake off the surplus water, and lay the paper, painting surface up, on a drawing board, preferably of a size that gives 2in (5cm) clearance all around from the margin of the paper. Stick the edges down with strips from a roll of brown paper tape. Put a thumbtack in each corner. As the painting paper dries, it will pull itself smooth and tight.

For field work, some artists use a light panel of wood or masonite smaller than the cut paper. Two or three sheets of dampened paper are laid over the thin board, folded down and under, and held in place with a number of spring clips. The toughness of the dried, stretched paper holds it in place when the clips are removed; and a completed sheet can be taken off without disturbing the lower sheets.

Ready-prepared watercolor boards — light papers mounted on cardboard — are pleasant to use and do not, of course, need stretching. But they are more expensive than paper and heavy to carry in quantity.

Home-made boards, with light paper strongly glued to pasteboard, can be satisfactory for practice; but paper should always be glued to the back of these boards to prevent buckling.

Special stretching-frames can be bought, onto which heavier weights of paper can be stretched and held taut, with the edges crimped between an inner and an outer framework. These are for experts, providing a pleasant "give" to the paper similar to that of an oil canvas. But even experts have been known to hole their wash-weakened paper; and some artists believe that such stretching adversely affects the surface texture of the paper.

Manufacturers often produce small swatches of paper samples, which enable the artist to compare the different weights and textures of the various types. Because the quality papers are quite expensive, there may be a charge for a sample swatch, but it is very useful reference material for artists working mainly in watercolor.

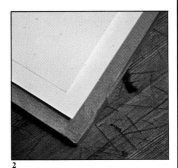
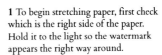

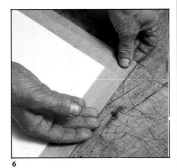

1 To begin stretching paper, first check which is the right side of the paper. Hold it to the light so the watermark appears the right way around.

2 Trim the paper to size for the drawing board, leaving a good margin of board so that the gummed tape will adhere.

3 Soak the paper in a tray or sink full of clean water. The amount of time needed to soak varies with the type of paper.

4 Measure out lengths of gummed paper tape to match each side of the drawing board.

5 Take the paper out of water and drain it off. Lay it on the board and stick dampened gummed tape along one side.

6 Stick gum strip along the opposite side of the paper. Tape the other two sides. Keep the paper quite flat throughout.

7 To secure the paper, push a thumbtack into the board at each corner. Let the paper dry naturally or it may split.

EQUIPMENT

Paints

In the case of watercolors, price more accurately reflects quality than it does in any other medium. Large, cheap multi-hued boxes of so-called watercolor — muddy, impermanent, and consisting more of filler than pigment — may delight the eye of a child but are useless for serious work. "Students' Colors," usually put in smaller boxes or in tube-color sets, are good for practice, especially if made by a reputable firm. But only those paints labeled "Artists' Colors" can be relied upon to give the transparency, glow, and permanence that the keen artist, professional or amateur, requires.

In this expensive, hightest-quality range, there is no essential difference — except in terms of portability and convenience — between "solid" and tube colors. The quality names to keep in mind are Winsor and Newton, Rowney, Schmincke Horadam, and Grumbacher.

Dry cakes and semi-moist pans are little used nowadays; half-pans, also semi-moist, are the best-known form. The best-quality half-pans can be bought singly in their tiny white boxes, and are often sold as sets in small flat boxes which double as palettes.

Semi-liquid tubes of watercolor are preferred by artists who wish to apply large washes. Fully liquid watercolor can be bought in bottles, with an eye-dropper provided to transfer paint to palette. Good ranges include Luma and Dr. Martin's. It is obviously quicker to use these, or the watered-down "liquid" tube color, than to lift color from a half-pan with a wet brush to make up a wash.

Few watercolor artists, even the most expert, would claim to use more than 11 or 12 colors, from which the whole range could be mixed. But early English watercolorists, like Thomas Girtin, painted masterpieces using a palette of no more than five basic, permanent colors. There is certainly no need for any artist to keep any more than 10 or 11 colors.

An adequate modern palette is: ivory black, Payne's gray (optional), burnt umber, cadmium red, yellow ochre, cadmium yellow, Hooker's green, viridian, monastral blue, French ultramarine, and Alizarin crimson.

Professional artists may argue about the "best" basic palette, but few would disagree that a beginner or early student is best advised to stick to a restricted palette, which not only forces him or her to consider the basics of color mixing but imposes a pleasing harmony and consistency on the finished work.

Some pigments with a chemical dye base will stain paper, rather than create a transparent wash on the surface. The "stainers," which might be quite useful for certain purposes, can be quite easily discovered: blob the color on paper and let it dry. Then rinse under running water. "Stain" pigments will remain.

Purists — and experimenters — can make their own watercolors at home or in the studio — a time-consuming process, but some may find it worthwhile. They will need finely-ground pigments of the finest quality, a plate glass slab, a grinding miller or muller, a plastic palette knife or spatula, and gum arabic, glycerin, distilled water, ox gall, sugar solution, and carbolic acid solution.

Pour one part of mixed sugar and glycerin solution plus two or three parts of gum arabic and a few drops of ox gall into a little pool on the glass. Then, with the palette knife, slowly draw in and mix the little heap of pigment placed beside it until there is a stiff paste.

Brushes

The patient craft of the brushmaker is tested to the full in making brushes that meet the demands of watercolor artists. They want flat or chisel-edged brushes that lay good even washes, and brushes that can be drawn to a fine point to render detail as well as lay a lot of color in one even stroke.

In the various sizes that are also demanded, the nearest to a perfect bristle that the brushmakers have found is red sable, from the tail hairs of Siberian mink. These make the most expensive but the longest-lasting of brushes, providing they are well cared-for.

Squirrel or Japanese pony (so-called "camel") hair are the best substitutes. Man-made fibers — synthetics — have still to make an adequate mark as far as artists are concerned.

The very fine brushes (000, 00, and 0) are rarely used. Fine is considered to start with 1, going through to 12. A beginner's range might well start with 4, 8, and 12 in the "rounds," plus a $\frac{1}{2}$in or 1in (1.25 or 2.5cm) flat. The choice depends on what the artist needs to do.

Chinese hogshair brushes are now available in the West; these are long-handled (bamboo), with the bristles tightly bunched for delicate, fine-point work.

Easels

There are many types of easel, most of which can be set and adjusted for watercolor work. The delicate — it might almost be described as intimate — work of watercolor is best carried out at close quarters, either on a board mounted surface, propped up on a table in the studio, or rested on the knee, or on a light, specialized easel in the field.

Watercolor easels range from the neck strap and board for sketching to well-patented collapsible wood and aluminum contraptions, to the satchel that converts to an outdoor stool.

Water

In materials, consider the water the most important adjunct of all. Use distilled water whenever possible. Over-hard or too soft water can play strange tricks with paper and colors. Carry the water in a large screw-top bottle if painting outdoors; and tip it into two jars — one for washing the brushes, one for slaking the colors: delicate tints can easily be muddied by using water in which brushes have ween washed.

Watercolors are available in sets as well as in individual pans or tubes. Half pans (back, center and center left) can be purchased both individually and in sets. The boxes (left and right) can easily double as palettes. Bottled, concentrated watercolors (center) usually have an eyedropper applicator. Tube colors (front, back) just need to be squeezed onto the palette before being used.

A wide range of watercolors is available, and the manufacturers produce charts of all colors available in each range (▶). It is common to find that a single manufacturer may produce more than one range, one of which will be more expensive and better quality than the others. The lower quality ranges are produced by avoiding the use of expensive pigments, and usually an attempt is made to standardize prices. There will be differences also between the flow and permanence of the different-quality paints. Soft sable brushes are best for most techniques, and these are produced in different series by several manufacturers. This selection of size 5 brushes from different series (▼) indicates the variations. The brushes are (from left to right): Proarte Series 1 and 3, LP Series 38, Winsor and Newton Series 7, LP Series 1A, Winsor and Newton Series 3A, 16, and 33. The Winsor and Newton Series 7 is the highest quality red sable brush available.

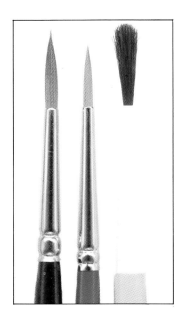

Many watercolor boxes include a brush, but these are often of very poor quality, as can be seen (◀) in a comparison (from left to right) between a best quality sable brush, a synthetic sable, and the extremely cheap type of brush sometimes found in boxes. The series of brushes (▶) shows all the different sizes available in one type of brush. Japanese bamboo brushes (▼ top right) are versatile and convenient, both for covering large areas and for detailed work with the brush tip. A range of brushes suitable for watercolor painting are shown (▼) (from left to right): blender, fine synthetic roundhair, broad synthetic round hair, mixed fibers round, ox hair round, squirrel hair round, sable fan bright, sable round, fine sable round.

Watercolor painting techniques are traditionally associated with ink drawing and wash. To some extent, painting with stick inks combines the two types of work. Soft brushes are used, set in bamboo handles; they can be splayed out for broad sweeps of color or drawn up to a very fine point for line work. This small ink set (▶), produced by Grumbacher, gives one colored ink and black, and a fine bamboo brush. Several sizes of brush are available. The materials may be used in the manner of ink or watercolor, or combined with ordinary water-based paints.

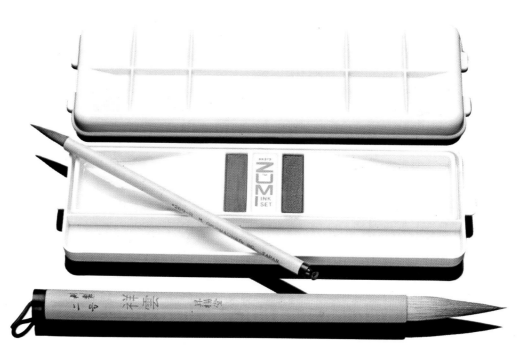

Since the characteristic feature of watercolor painting is the extreme liquidity of the paint, rags and sponges (◀) are very useful both as painting utensils and to control or mop up the paint if it runs too much. Paint dabbed on with a sponge has a rich, rough texture.

The essential feature of watercolor painting, which makes it different from other techniques, is that the color values are reduced only by the addition of water, never by adding white paint, and the paint is thus always transparent. These two examples of different dilutions of watercolor paint (▶) serve to illustrate this point. A strong hue may be applied to the paper by adding only enough water to the paint to make it flow evenly. The traditional watercolor technique, however, is to allow the strength of the color to build up in the painting by successive applications of thin washes of dilute, transparent color, leaving bare patches of paper for white highlights. The brilliance of the white paper also emerges through the thin layers, which gives watercolors their clarity and luminosity.

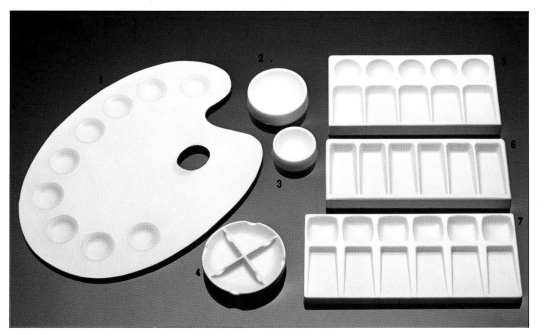

Recessed or well palettes must be used for mixing watercolor, so that any quantity of water required can be added and colors cannot flow together. Palettes of ceramic material, plastic, or metal are suitable, and are available in a variety of different sizes and shapes. It is really a matter of personal choice whether a separate small cup (2, 3) is used for each color, or whether the paints are kept together in a large palette with several wells (4, 5, 6, 7). The traditional kidney-shaped palette with a thumb hole (1), which can be held in the hand while painting, may be more useful for outdoor work, where flat surfaces may not be available, but for studio work no one style is more valuable than another. If extra palette room is needed, ordinary plates and saucers are quite suitable, and the paint is easily washed away afterward.

Before buying an easel the watercolorist should give careful consideration to his or her requirements. A large variety of easels is now available, so the artist should be able to find a suitable one without difficulty. The best studio easels can be adjusted to a horizontal position for sketching. Many watercolorists work outside. For this type of painting, some artists prefer to work with only a drawing board and pad, but there are many collapsible lightweight easels that are also suitable. Some portable easels are provided with a compartment for carrying materials. Generally, aluminum easels are cheaper than wooden ones. However, since these easels are very light,

it is advisable to buy one that has spikes on the feet to hold the easel firm in windy conditions or on soft ground. The sketching easel (1) has rubber tipped feet, but it can be supplied with spikes if required. It is made from beechwood, a very hard-wearing wood. The adjustable legs enable the artist to work at a comfortable height. When fully extended this easel will hold a canvas at a fixed height, either in a vertical position or tilted forward to any desired angle. It is easy to carry, weighing only 3¼lbs (1.6kg). The aluminum sketching easel (2) is slightly larger. It is fully adjustable. A disadvantage of this easel is that it has only rubber feet, which will not always

keep the easel steady. The aluminum table easel (3) is extremely light. When not in use it folds up very compactly and can be stored out of the way.The radial studio easel (4) is made of wood, and it can also be folded to take up less space. The easel may be tilted backward and forward, as can the canvas, which can also be moved to a horizontal position. There is an extra large wing nut to lock the easel steady. The combination easel (5), made of seasoned beechwood, is both a folding studio easel and a drawing table. This makes it extremely practical for artists who have small studios. It will take a very wide canvas, tilted at any angle or kept in an upright position. When it is

1

2

3

4

used as a drawing table, the frame for the
drawing board can be adjusted easily to a
comfortable height. The frame will hold
drawing boards of any standard size or
type. A useful piece of equipment for
artists who work outdoors is the
combined satchel and stool (**6**). A strap is
attached to the light metal legs of the
stool so that it is easy to carry. All the
artist's materials, such as paints, brushes,
and paper, can be put in the satchel.
Another easel for outdoor work is the
combined sketching seat and easel (**7**).
This versatile easel can be used with
canvas, block, frame, and sketching
board. It is fully adjustable, and is easily
carried by the handle attached to the seat.

If the artist is sketching a moving
subject, a drawing board with a strap
attached may well prove useful. The
strap is passed around the artist's neck,
leaving the hands free for
work and allowing him
or her to walk
around.

CHAPTER TWO

Technique

LAYING A FLAT WASH

Pure watercolor, being transparent, must be applied from light to dark. The paper itself is used to create the pure white or light tones which, with opaque paints, would be made by using white alone or mixed with colored pigment.

Any area required to be white is simply "reserved," or left unpainted, so that when it is surrounded with darker washes it will shine out with great brilliance. Pale tones are created in the same way, with a light-colored wash put on first and then surrounded with darker tones. Light reflected off the paper, back through these thin skins of paint known as washes, gives a watercolor painting a spontaneity and sparkle which cannot be achieved with any other medium. Hence watercolor's popularity with artists both past and present.

The two most important facts about watercolor are, first, that it is always to some extent unpredictable, even in the hands of experts, and, second, that because dark is always worked over light, some planning is needed before beginning the painting. It is not always necessary to do a detailed and complicated drawing on the paper, only

enough to work out the basic shapes and design; this really should be done, however, or you will begin without really knowing which areas are to be left white or pale and how they will fit into the painting as a whole.

Thus the first step in any painting is to establish where the first wash is to be applied; and the first step in watercolor technique is to learn how to put on the wash.

The wash is the basis of all watercolor painting, whether it is a broad, sweeping one, covering a large expanse, such as a sky or the background to a portrait, or a much smaller one laid on a particular area. Washes need not be totally flat. They can be gradated in both tone and color, or broken up and varied. But the technique of laying a flat wash must be mastered, even if you subsequently find that you seldom use it.

The support should be tilted at a slight angle so that the brush strokes flow into one another, but do not run down the paper. For a broad wash a large chisel-edged brush is normally used; for a smaller one, or a wash which is to be laid against a complicated edge, a smaller round brush may be more manageable. Laying a wash must be done quickly or hard edges will form between brush strokes.

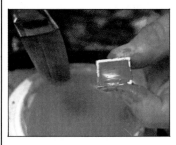 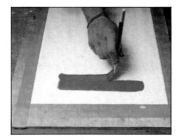 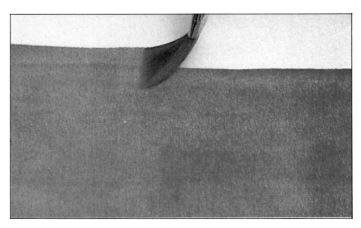

A flat wash in a vivid color is being laid on dampened paper with a broad, flat-ended brush. it is not strictly necessary to dampen the paper (many artists prefer the slightly "dragged" look given by working on dry paper), but dampening

facilitates an even covering. Tilt the board slightly so that the brush strokes flow into one another, and work backward and forward down the paper until the whole area is covered.

Therefore mix up more paint than you think you will need. Start by damping the paper with clear water (this is not actually essential, but helps the paint to go on evenly). Working in one direction, lay a horizontal line of color at the top of the area, then another below it, working in the opposite direction, and continue working in alternate directions until the area is covered. Never go back over the wet paint because you feel it is uneven or not dark enough, as this will result in the paint's "flooding" and leave blobs and patches. A final word of caution: if the doorbell or the telephone rings while you are in the middle of a wash, ignore it; otherwise you will return to a hard edge which is impossible, or at least very difficult, to remove.

Leave the wash to dry before working on adjacent areas of the

painting. Not until the wash is completely dry will you be able to establish either how even it is or what its true color value is (watercolor dries much paler than it appears when wet). The ability to assess the precise tone of a wash comes only with experience, but it can be helpful to lay down one or two patches of flat color on a spare piece of paper and allow them to dry as a preliminary test. Washes can be laid on top of the first one to strengthen the color or darken the tone, though too many will turn the painting muddy. Purists claim that more than three layers spoil the quality.

Another method of laying a wash is to use a sponge. This is particularly useful when a slightly variegated or textured wash is required, as the sponge can either be filled with paint for a dense covering or used relatively dry for a paler effect. A sponge can also be used in conjunction with a brush. If, for instance, you rinse it in clean water and squeeze it out, you can remove some of the paint laid by a brush while it is still wet, thus lightening selected areas — a good technique for skies or distant hills.

Often a wash needs to be slightly textured or varied in strength, for which purpose a sponge is useful.

1 The wash is mixed with a brush and tested on a piece of spare paper.

2 Enough paint is mixed to cover the area, and the sponge is dipped into it. For a lighter covering, some of the paint can be squeezed out.

3 A variegated effect is achieved by applying the paint quite thickly with the first stroke, much more thinly with the second.

4 The final wash can be worked into with the sponge while it is still wet, in order to lighten some areas and produce a soft, shimmering effect.

A sponge can be used to lighten paint applied by brush. A brush can also be used to add detail to wet paint applied with a sponge as here.

1 The paper is dampened with a sponge, and a thin wash of color is applied, also with a sponge.

2 A second color is then flooded on, using the tip of the sponge so that the two run together.

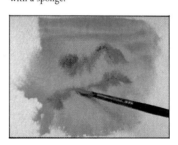

3 A brush is now used to touch in darker areas on the still-wet paint. Very subtle effects can be created by this wet-into-wet technique, but they are always to some extent unpredictable.

COMPLEX EDGES

Sometimes a wash must be laid against a complicated edge — for example, a group of roofs and chimneys with an intricate outline. The wash must then start from the edge, rather than end at it, which may necessitate turning the board sideways or upside down. When dampening the paper, take care to dampen only up to this edge; otherwise the wash will flow into the areas to be reserved.

This kind of technical problem highlights the need for initial planning — the success of a painting may hinge on the precise way a certain area has been outlined by reserving. Another method for dealing with intricate shapes is to stop out the parts to be reserved with liquid mask.

GRADATED AND VARIEGATED WASHES

Colors in nature are seldom totally flat or one solid hue. It is often desirable, therefore, to lay a gradated wash, which becomes darker or lighter at the top or bottom or changes from one color to another. For a gradated wash, simply mix more water with the paint to make each successive strip lighter, or more pigment to darken them.

For a variegated wash, mix up the two or more colors to be used, dampen the paper as usual, and then lay on the colors so that they blend into one another. The effect of such a wash cannot be worked out precisely in advance, even with practice — you should be prepared for a happy (or unhappy) accident. As with a flat wash, even if you are

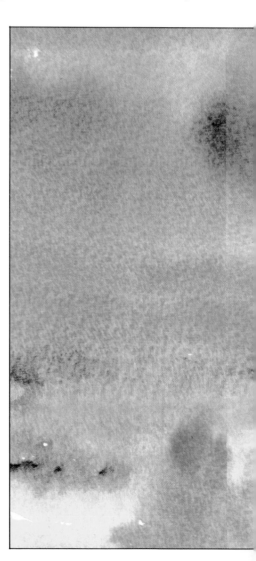

unhappy with the result never make corrections while the paint is still wet; if you are dissatisfied when it is dry it can be sponged out and a another wash laid on top.

Some watercolorists use variegated washes in a particularly free way. Each individual arrives at his own technique by trial and error. Attractive efforts can sometimes be achieved by deliberately allowing the paint to flood in the middle of a wash, by introducing blobs of strong color to a paler wash while the paint is damp, or by laying one wash over a dry one, thus producing a slight granulation of the paper. Such effects are unpredictable. For one thing, they vary widely according to the type of paper used and its absorbency. But one of the great joys of watercolor is the opportunity it provides for turning accidental effects to advantage.

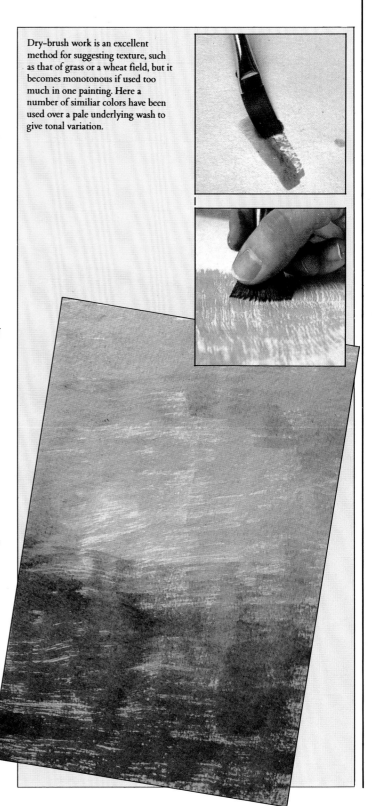

Dry-brush work is an excellent method for suggesting texture, such as that of grass or a wheat field, but it becomes monotonous if used too much in one painting. Here a number of similiar colors have been used over a pale underlying wash to give tonal variation.

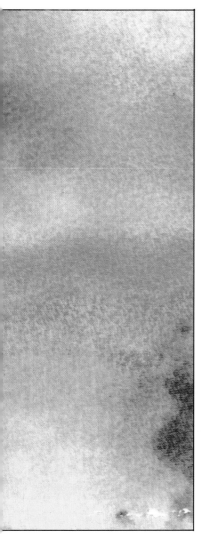

(◀)Prussian blue and alizarin crimson have been allowed to run into one another, just as they would with a wash of only one color. Such effects are impossible to control accurately; the artist must be prepared for an element of "happy accident."

(◀ ◀)Laying one wash on top of another often gives textural variety as well as intensifying the color. Notice that the bottom band, a pale wash of Payne's grey, is quite even, while the one at the top, a third application of the same wash, shows distinct brush marks.

(◀ ◀ ◀)The possibilities of working wet-into-wet may be explored by producing this kind of doodle in a matter of minutes. The wet-into-wet technique is often used in the early stages of a painting, or for the background — more precise work being done at a later stage or in another area of the painting.

DRY-BRUSH AND TEXTURAL METHODS

Painting with a small amount of paint on a fine brush which is almost dry is a method most frequently used for the fine details of a painting, but dry-brush is also a technique in its own right and can be used very effectively for large areas, either over a wash that has already been laid down or straight onto white paper. For landscape work it can be used to suggest the texture of grass, trees, rocks, stone walls, and the like. For portraits and still-lifes it can model forms more easily than washes of wet paint can.

Like all watercolor techniques, dry-brush requires practice. If the paint is too wet it will go on as a solid wash; if too dry it will not go on at all. The brush normally used for large areas of dry-brush work is a large chisel-edged type, with the bristles slightly splayed to produce a series of fine lines, somewhat like hatching and cross-hatching in drawing. One color and tone can be laid over another, and the brush strokes can be put on in different directions as the shape suggests.

The Victorian artist William Holman Hunt (1827-1910) used this method extensively, together with stippling, in which small dots of color are applied to the paper very close together, similar to the way that the French artist Georges Seurat (1859-91) applied oil paint.

Scumbling is a method of applying fairly thick paint in a circular scrubbing motion so that the paint goes onto the paper from all directions and picks up the texture of the surface. It is effective when

1 When spattering with a mask, the artist uses detail paper to trace the area he wants to mask.

2 He then carefully cuts the mask with an X-Acto knife.

4 More sap green, again mixed with gum water, is spattered on the area with an ordinary household brush.

5 The slightly irregular stippled effect is clear, even before the mask is peeled off.

used for relatively small areas to provide contrast to flat washes, but if used too extensively in one painting it can become monotonous.

Another common method of suggesting texture is to spatter wet paint onto the paper with a toothbrush or bristle-brush. This technique, too, should be reserved for certain areas only, but it is an excellent way of dealing with a pebble beach, say, or a rough stone wall. The paint is usually spattered over an existing wash, not directly onto white paper, and to make the result look natural, care must be taken to use paint that is not much darker than the wash. Mask off surrounding areas if they are lighter in tone.

Masking tape can be used for a straight edge; however for more complex shapes, a rough mask can be cut from drawing paper.

Liquid mask provides a way of painting in "negative," which can give very subtle and exciting effects.

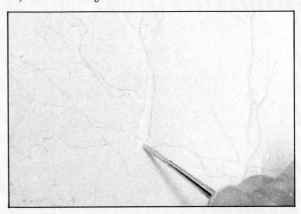

1 The areas to be masked are carefully drawn, and the fluid is applied with a fine brush.

2 The fluid is allowed to dry and a yellow-brown wash is laid over the top.

3 The mask is applied and the tree is painted in sap green, mixed with a little gum water to give it extra body and brilliance.

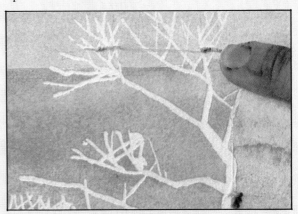

3 A blue wash for the sky is added and allowed to dry, after which the fluid is peeled off by gentle rubbing with a finger.

6 The mask is removed, leaving a sharp, clean outline. The slightly irregular texture is very effective in suggesting foliage.

MASKING OUT AND CREATING HIGHLIGHTS

Many watercolorists use liquid mask and masking tape for reserving areas of white paper. Liquid mask, which is specially made for the purpose, is a kind of liquid rubber sold in small bottles and applied with a brush. Purists disdain to use it, but their scorn is baseless. Very attractive and exciting effects, quite different from those produced by the classic method of laying washes around an area, can be gained with it. Stopping out with liquid mask is a method of painting in "negative"; the precise and subtle shades made by the brush remain when the liquid mask is removed.

The paper must be quite dry before the liquid mask is applied, and the liquid mask itself must be allowed to dry before a wash is laid on top. Once the wash has dried, the mask can be rubbed off with a finger or a soft eraser, leaving the white area, which can be modified and worked into if desired. Liquid mask should never be left on the paper for longer than necessary, and care must be taken to wash the brushes immediately; otherwise fluid will harden in the hairs and ruin them. Liquid mask is not suitable for all papers, especially ones with a rough surface. The technique is illustrated on page 23.

Masking tape is particularly useful for straight-edged areas, such as the light-catching side of a building or the edge of a window-sill. There is no reason why all painting should be done freehand; just as few people can draw a circle without recourse to compass, few people can paint a really straight line without smudging paint over the edge. Masking tape enables you to use the paint freely without worrying about spoiling the area to be reserved.

Yet another way of keeping the paint off part of the paper is to use wax, in what is called the resist method, like that used in batik fabrics. This differs from the previous techniques in being permanent; once the wax is on the paper it cannot be removed except by laborious scraping with a razor blade. The paint, moreover, will lie on top of the wax to some extent (this varies according to the paper used), leaving a slightly textured surface. The effect can be attractive, particularly for flowers or fabrics. An ordinary household candle can be used, or a white wax crayon for finer lines.

The best method of creating fine, delicate highlights when a painting is nearly complete is to scrape into the paint with a sharp point, of an X-Acto knife, say, so that the white paper is revealed. Very fine lines can be drawn in this way to suggest a blade of grass or a flower stem catching the light in the foreground of a landscape. Such touches often give a painting that extra something it seems to need. They can also be achieved by applying Chinese white with a fine brush, but scraping back tends to give a cleaner line.

(▲)Watercolor has been used in conjunction with pastel to give liveliness and textural contrast to this painting. Both the building itself and the dark tree on the left are in pure watercolor, while the foreground grass is pure pastel. The sky is a combination of the two. Pastel combines well with watercolor, and a painting such as this often benefits from a "non-purist" approach.

(▼)Sharp, clean lines and highlights can be made by scraping into dry paint with an X-Acto knife or other sharp knife. Take care not to damage the paper by pressing too hard.

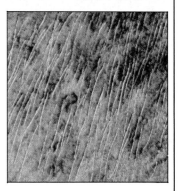

MIXING MEDIA

Many other media can be used in combination with watercolor; indeed, the mixing of media is now commonplace, whereas in the past it was regarded as breaking the rules. Watercolor used with pen and ink has a long history; in the days before watercolor became recognized as a medium in its own right, it was used mainly to give touches of color to drawings or to tint black and white engravings. Nowadays there are many other media – some old and some new – that can be used with watercolor to good effect.

One traditional way to change the nature of paint by thickening it is to mix it with a little gum arabic, which gives it both texture and lasting luster. Soap can be used in much the same way, and it makes the paint easier to scrape back. Soap can also be used to make imprints of objects such as leaves or flowers. Coat the object with soap, apply paint to it, and then press it onto the paper.

Watercolors can be drawn into with pens, pencils, crayons, or pastels, and areas can be stressed or lightened with gouache or Chinese white. Watercolor pencils and crayons, a relatively new invention, are particularly suitable for this purpose. When dry they behave like crayons or hard pastels, but if dipped in water or used on wet paper they will dissolve, forming a wash. Using these, or ordinary pastels, on top of watercolor can turn a painting that has "gone wrong" and become dull and lifeless into something quite new and different. It is always worthwhile experimenting with such media on a painting that you are less than happy with; you may evolve a personal technique that you can use again. Wax oil pastels can create interesting textured areas when laid underneath a wash, as can treating the paper, or parts of it, with mineral spirits before painting, which has a similar effect. The possibilities are almost endless, and experimentation is sure to reward you with interesting discoveries.

PROBLEM-SOLVING

Although watercolors cannot be altered so drastically or so often as paintings in any of the opaque media, changes are possible. It is a mistake to abandon a picture because a first wash has gone wrong.

The first thing to remember is that a wash that looks too dark or too vivid on a sheet of otherwise white paper will dry much lighter and may look quite pale when surrounded by other colors. If the first wash looks wrong, let it dry. If you are still quite sure it is not what you intended, sponge it out with a clean sponge and clear water. This may leave a slight stain on the paper, depending on the paper used and the color itself (some colors stain the paper, like a dye, while other do not), but when dry it will be too faint to spoil the new wash. When a wash has flooded, sponge it out immediately without waiting for it to dry; flooding cannot be entirely remedied, though it can sometimes

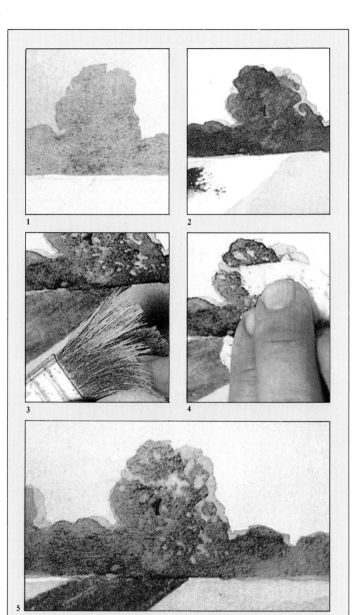

Gum water, which is gum arabic diluted in water, adds richness to watercolors and keeps the colors bright. It can also be used, as here, as a sort of resist method to create highlights.

1 The tree and hedge are painted in with pure watercolor.

2 A further wash of green is applied, this time mixed with gum water.

3 The area of the central tree is spattered with water, flicked on with a household brush.

4 The central tree is blotted with a rag, so that wherever the water has touched, small areas of paint are lifted off, the gum being soluble in water.

5 The lighter patches of color give an extra sparkle to the tree, while the addition of the gum water imparts richness to the dark green on either side.

create an effect not originally planned.

One of the commonest faults is accidentally to take a wash over the edge of an area to be reserved. There are three ways of dealing with this, depending on the size of the area and the type of edge desired. If the wash is pale and the area to be reserved is a broad and imprecise shape, such as a stone in the foreground of a landscape, you can simply sponge out the excess paint with a small sponge or absorbent cotton dampened in clean water. A soft edge will be left. For a more intricate shape, or one requiring a sharp, clear edge, you may have to scrape the paint away (after it is dry) with a razor blade or X-Acto knife, the former for broad areas, the latter for small ones. Hold the blade flat on the paper so that the corners do not dig in, and scrape gently. The same method can be used to lighten an area or to create texture by removing a top layer of paint. The third rescue technique - - to apply Chinese white with a fine brush — should be used only when the painting is otherwise complete; if the white is allowed to mix with other colors it will muddy them and spoil the translucency.

The small blots and smudges that often occur when you take a loaded brush over a painting or rest your hand on a still-damp area can also be razored out when dry. If a splash of paint or dirty water falls on the painting, quickly soak up the excess with a twist of tissue or a cotton swab, let it dry, and then razor it out gently. If you are intending to apply more paint to the area, rub it down lightly with a soft eraser to smooth the surface.

Even professionals sometimes find that a painting has gone so wrong that small corrections will not suffice or has become so clogged with paint that further work is impossible. If this happens, you can throw it away, or you can also wash out the whole painting, or large parts of it, by putting the paper under running water and sponging the surface. Leave it on its board if you have stretched it. A slight stain may be left, and its faint shadow will serve as a drawing for the next attempt. A whole sky or foreground can be removed in this way, while leaving intact those areas with which you are satisfied.

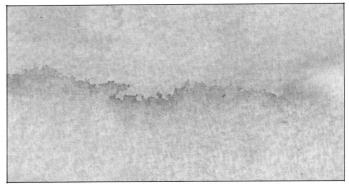

One of the attractions of watercolor is that new uses of the medium are often supported by "mistakes."

A wash that has "gone wrong" (▲) and flooded, has been worked into to create a sky effect not originally planned (▼).

· CHAPTER THREE ·

Figures

INTRODUCTION

Watercolor is commonly believed to be suited only to certain subjects. It is "perfect" for landscape, of course, and possible for flowers, but surely it is much too uncontrollable to be brought to the service of figure and portrait painting. It is true that there is no strong tradition of figure work in watercolor and that all the most famous paintings of people — those we see in art collections — are in oils, but this has nothing to do with any inherent unsuitability of the medium. The reason for the choice of oils is a much simpler one. In the past, most paintings were done for a fee, and artists had to please their patrons. Those who were wealthy enough to commission a portrait or pay a high price for a nude study wanted a large, imposing painting that would stand the ravages of time, and this meant one in oils.

Nowadays, however, we paint for ourselves and do not have to produce highly finished work with every hair or jewel described in faithful detail. More and more artists are finding that watercolor is a marvelous medium for figure and portrait work, ideal for freer, more impressionistic treatments, and perfectly suited for capturing impressions of light and the delicate, living qualities of skin and hair.

Drawing

No branch of painting is problem-free, and because watercolors cannot be re-worked and corrected to any great extent, it is vital to start a painting on a good foundation. This means that before you can paint figures or faces successfully you must first be able to draw them.

The best way to approach the complexities of the human figure is to see it as a set of simple forms that fit together — the ovoid of the head joining the cylinder of the neck, which in turn, fits into the broader, flatter planes of the shoulders, and so on. If you intend to tackle the whole figure, avoid the temptation to begin with small details; instead, map out the whole figure first in broad lines.

Proportion is particularly important, and many promising paintings are spoiled by a too-large head or feet that could not possibly be used for their proper function because they are much too small for the body. The best way to check proportions is to hold up a pencil to the subject and slide your thumb up and down it to measure the various elements. This will quickly show you the size of a hand in relation to a forearm and the ratio of head-width to shoulder-width.

Another way to improve your drawing is to look not at the forms themselves, but at the spaces between them. If a model is standing with one arm resting on a hip, there will be a space of a particular shape between these forms. Draw this, not the arm itself, and then move on to any other "negative shapes" you can see. This method is surprisingly accurate.

Composition

It is easy to become so bogged down in the intricacies of the human figure and face that composition is forgotten, but it is every bit as important as in any other branch of painting. Even if you are painting just a head-and-shoulder portrait, always give thought to the placing of the head within the square or rectangle of the paper, the background, and the balance of tones.

A plain light-colored wall might be the ideal foil for a dark-haired sitter, allowing you to concentrate the drama on the face itself, but you will often find you need more background or foreground interest to balance a subject. Placing your sitter in front of a window, for example, will give an interesting pattern of vertical and horizontal lines in the background as well as a subtle fall of light, while a chair or sofa not only serves the purpose of supporting the model but also provide, in its curved or straight lines, pictorial interest.

Figures or groups of figures in an outdoor setting require equally careful planning. You will need to think about whether to make them the focal point of the painting, where to place them in relation to the foreground and background, and what other elements you should include — or suppress. It is a good idea to make a series of small thumbnail sketches to work out the composition before you begin to paint.

Mother and Child by Greta Fenton.

This lovely, tender group should quickly
disabuse us of the notion that the figure
cannot be painted in watercolor. In the
right hands it is the perfect medium.
The artist has painted directly from life,
working mainly wet-in-wet with a large
Chinese brush and adding definition
with delicate red crayon lines.

PORTRAIT OF PAUL

This sensitive study is much more graphic in approach than the previous portrait. The artist is more interested in line than in color, and has used a technique that is a combination of drawing and painting, enabling her to express the character of the sitter in a way she found suited his thin, somewhat aquiline, features.

She used a quill pen made from a goose feather, a drawing tool much favored by such artists as Rembrandt, but the medium was dilute watercolor instead of the more traditional ink. A quill pen produces a less mechanical line than a metal nib, because strokes of different thickness can be made by turning the quill. By this means, and by varying the strength and colors of the paint itself, the artist has produced a series of contrasting lines — some thick and soft, some short and stabbing, and some fine and taut. She used a Chinese brush in combination with the quill, both to lay washes across the whole image and to soften the line in places by dipping it in a little clean water. Watercolor gives artists more freedom to modify or alter lines.

1 A simple pose, seen directly from the front, was chosen for the painting, because it gave the artist the opportunity to explore fully the lines and contours of the features. No preliminary pencil drawing was made, since the painting was in itself a drawing, which could be corrected as the work progressed.

30

2 This photograph shows how the artist varied the strength of the watercolor when drawing with the quill. She used three different mixtures: raw sienna and cobalt blue; Prussian blue and cadmium red; and yellow ochre and cadmium yellow.

3 Here the artist has found that she is not satisfied with the line of the cheekbone; so she lightens it with a brush dipped in water before redrawing it.

4 A Chinese brush was used to apply small areas of color all over the image. No attempt was made to render the colors precisely; they were applied in a spontaneous manner to create an overall effect.

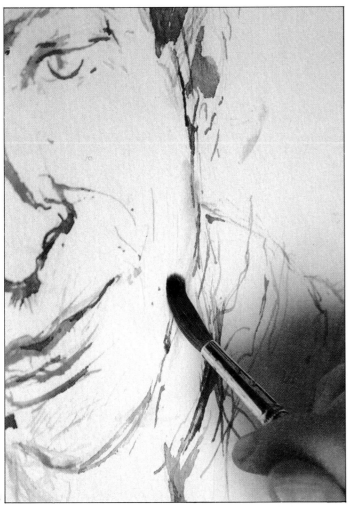

5

6

5 The artist has made little use of the traditional watercolor technique of flat washes. Instead, she has allowed the brushmarks to become part of the painting. The background was applied with two different brushes, a No. 9 sable round and a Chinese brush.

6 Once the lines had been firmly established and the artist was satisfied with the drawing, she laid a loose wash over the face and neck to build up the form and add warmth to the flesh.

Portrait of Paul.

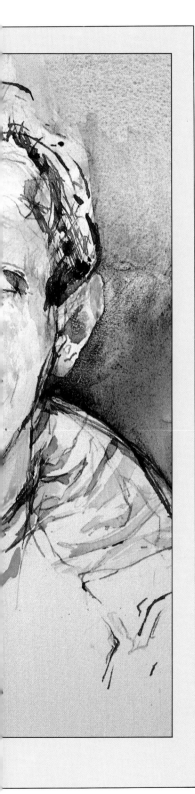

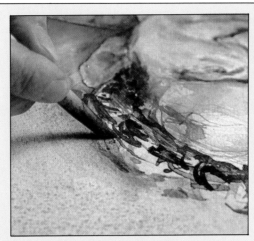 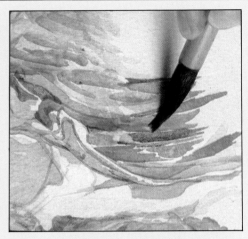

Although color is not the most important aspect of the painting, it has been used boldly and sensitively. Here the artist is using a Chinese brush to apply small patches of bright color to the clothing and darker tones to the hair.

Sir Geraint Evans by Richard Willis.

In this carefully observed and strongly drawn study, a preliminary sketch for an oil portrait of the renowned Welsh opera singer, the artist has explored the structure of the head through directional brushstrokes.

GIRL BY A WINDOW WITH A BLIND

In this painting the figure is seen in the context of an interior, and the effects of light interested the artist most. Watercolor has been used very loosely in thin washes, with a large amount of paper left uncovered, and the impression of a large, spacious room lit by diffused light has been created with minimal attention to detail. Although the paint has been used mainly pure, the artist also used gouache in the final stages for certain areas such as the blue bed and the smaller highlights on the face and body. Gouache can destroy the quality of a watercolor by giving a mate, dead surface, but here it has been used very skillfully without detriment to the painting.

The composition, with its careful arrangement of lights and darks, is well balanced. The crisp, diagonal lines of the blind contrast with the softer contours of the model, who is placed in silhouette against the white wall. It is the relationship between the figure and the window that gives the painting its interest, and the two are unified by the expanse of bright blue formed by the bed, which is in turn echoed by the cushion and shadow behind the model.

1 The artist has deliberately chosen the pose to fit in with a pre-conceived composition, and he was sufficiently sure of the placing of the main shapes not to need a preliminary pencil drawing. Instead, the main lines and shapes were mapped out with much-diluted watercolor.

2 The tree just visible through the slats of the blind was painted in very freely over the orange-brown lines of the blind. The darker lines thus show through the green wash, giving the shimmering effect of light striking the soft, uneven form of the tree.

3 The next step was to lay a dark gray-blue wash at the top of the window area, leaving white below so that the light was channeled through the bottom part of the window. The body was then established with a strong cadmium orange, balanced by the crimson of the skirt and the blue of the bed.

4 The artist continued to work all over the painting, modeling the outstretched leg and adding definition to the face and neck. A strong tint of raw sienna was used for the darker flesh tints in order to echo the orange-brown of the blind and window frame.

3

1

2

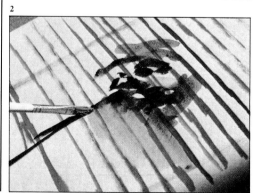

4

6

Girl by a Window with a Blind.

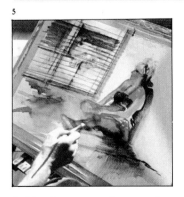

5

6 As a final touch, a deep pink flesh-tint was put on the body, and the area of the bed was strengthened by using a wash of blue gouache with white added. Too much use of gouache with watercolor can destroy its quality, but here it has been used skillfully.

5 Although pure watercolor was used for most of the painting, some white gouache was added for the smaller highlights, such as those on the leg and face.

BLOWING BUBBLES

This portrait, in which the artist has transformed a small snapshot into a finished watercolor, relies heavily on skilled use of certain specific techniques.

The photograph was of the whole figure of the child blowing bubbles, and of the background houses and Jungle gym, but the artist used only the upper left-hand corner containing the top part of the child's figure. She overlaid the photograph with a tracing paper grid in order to transfer the image onto a larger scale drawing on another piece of tracing paper. The grid divided the smaller image into 16 squares, and the artist then drew a larger version of each square, thus enlarging the whole scale. Taking the new drawing on tracing paper as a basis, the artist developed and corrected the image, using shading and detail to establish the accuracy of the outline.

Now it was time to transfer the drawing to white watercolor board. If she had done this in the usual way, by scribbling over the back of the tracing paper and then going over the outline of the impression with a pencil, she would have ended up with a gray outline and possibly smudges on the paper from the graphite pencil. She avoided this by using transfer paper, which is somewhat like office carbon paper but produces colored outlines. She placed this face downward on the support with the tracing paper drawing on top, and then carefully traced the outline with a leadholder (a special pencil into which a range of leads can be fitted, giving a fine, even line). This gave a faint image on the board.

The artist began the final painting by laying in a very diluted wash over the background and shadows of the face, hair, and clothing. This was almost the same color, with very little variation between the skin tones and background. She gradually introduced local color when building up with thin washes from light to dark in traditional watercolor manner. For this she used surgical brushes — brushes once used for examining people's eyes. These have the same adaptability and quality as small Chinese paint brushes.

1 A small snapshot is the only reference available to the artist for this watercolor portrait of a small child blowing bubbles.

2 Transfer paper is used to enlarge the photographic image to the required size. It is important to start with an absolutely accurate outline, and the artist takes particular care at this stage to obtain a clear, precise image.

3 Working on smooth watercolor board, the artist applies a wash of violet, Indian red, and yellow ochre to the background. This will be strengthened later.

4 The facial shadows are laid in a combination of the background colors. These are slightly darker than the background tone, and will give depth to subsequent washes

3

4

Enlarging the image

The basis for this watercolor portrait is a colored photograph. The artist first constructs a grid on a piece of tracing paper, to cover the relevant area of the photograph. A similar grid, the same size as the proposed painting, is then drawn on a second piece of tracing paper and the image enlarged square by square onto this. Any details to be included in the painting are also included in this enlarged drawing. A sheet of transfer paper is placed face down on the support. The enlarged drawing is laid on top of this and the artist carefully follows its lines. The transfer paper acts like carbon paper, producing a light brownish image (or other color, depending on the paper) which is ready for painting.

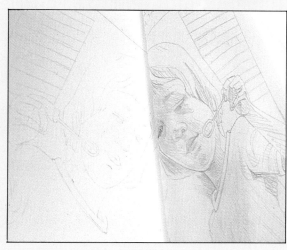

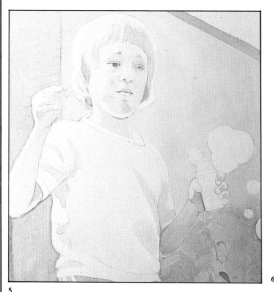

5

5 This initial wash can be applied with a fine sable brush, although our artist actually used a surgical brush, the type once used for examining eyes. This provides the artist with a quality and adaptability similar to that of small Chinese brushes

6

6 Shadows are touched in with the point of a No. 2 sable brush, in the traditional watercolor manner of dark over light. The artist moves across the image strengthening the tones — here the shadow between the hair and face is being darkened.

7 When painting details, the artist frequently finds it difficult to see enough information in the small photograph. The eye is touched in with the point of the No. 2 sable brush, but the artist feels the result is too dark, finding it necessary to strengthen some of the surrounding tones to compensate for this.

8 Most of the painting is built up from the three original colors — violet, yellow ochre, and Indian red — although small areas, such as the can of bubbles and the child's jeans, are added in the appropriate local color. To retain the harmony of the composition, the artist develops and strengthens the tones surrounding these brighter colors.

7

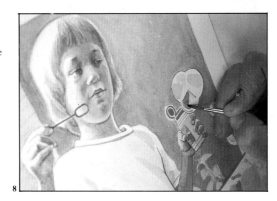

8

Blowing Bubbles.

38

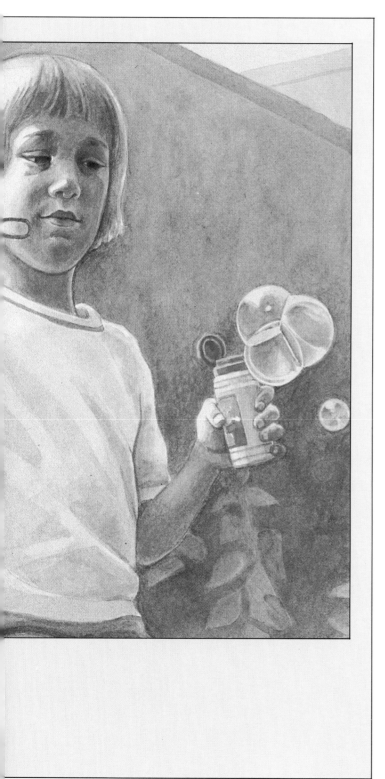

Be an opportunist

Anyone interested in painting their fellow humans should carry a sketchbook at all times and perhaps a watercolor box or watercolor crayons.

There are countless opportunities to draw and paint unobserved. Never attempt a detailed treatment, but try to grasp the essentials as quickly as you can, using any method you find you are happy with. Line and wash is much used for this kind of work, as is a combination of pencil and watercolor. You may find it easier to work in monochrome only, drawing with a brush and ink — an expressive and speedy way of conveying movement or blocking in areas of tone. If you do not use color, restrict yourself to the minimum, and don't bother about mixing the perfect subtle hue. If you want to use your sketches as reference for a later painting, make written notes about colors on each sketch.

Circus Cyclist by Jake Sutton.

Sutton draws with his brush to convey a marvelous sense of excitement and urgency. The variation in the brushstrokes, some like fine pencil scribbles and other swelling and tapering, seems to increase the momentum of the figure, propelling it forward, and adds to the feeling of imbalance.

AGAINST A STRIPED BLANKET

The artist worked from a live model to produce a watercolor in which the colors of the striped blanket in the background play a prominent role. The painting was done deliberately in a low color key, with the image built from loose washes across the paper surface. The brights have therefore been modified into softer pastel tones, yet work in relationship to each other. The charm of the portrait lies in these delicate differences between the overlapping areas of wash.

One of the main considerations in this work was to keep the model in an exact position, because the subtle light and shade tones on the face had to be stable in order for the slight differences to be seen. The model therefore had to be comfortable. She is sitting on a sofa, and the positions of her arms and feet — although not visible in the painting — were chalked so that she could resume the pose after rests.

She was also given a fixed point to look at.

The artist worked on a fairly large scale, almost life-size, which involved blocking in large areas of the paper. The character of the picture is very light, with even the striped blanket interpreted in subtle tones, and the bright blue shirt reduced to the palest shadows.

The first stage was a line drawing, but a minimal one consisting of the merest outline done with a leadholder to act as a guide. A very pale graded background wash was applied, starting with yellow and adding small quantities of cobalt blue as the artist moved from left to right. This gave a dimension to the background, so that it did not remain as a flat color but provided a spatial setting for the subject.

Hair often presents a problem to artists. It is difficult to decide whether to treat it as a mass — as one complete form — or to build it up as separate hairs, giving it an overall texture and trying to work in the many shapes within the main form. Here, the artist treated the tresses as separate forms, blocking in the shadow areas and highlights with fairly substantial wedges of color.

1 The artist draped a cheerful colored blanket over the back of the model's chair to brighten this portrait composition.

2 A lightly drawn sketch of the head, shoulders, and background is made on stretched Bockingford watercolor paper. The artist reworks the image, using a kneaded eraser where necessary, in order to get a good likeness of the model at this early stage. When the drawing is complete, the artist rubs out any dark lines, leaving an image that is clear enough to guide the painting, but which will not interfere with the delicate effects of subsequent watercolor washes.

3 When the drawing is complete, a highly diluted background wash is applied in order to eliminate some of the bright white expanse of paper. The artist begins with pale yellow on one side of the picture, adding small amounts of cobalt blue as she moves across the painting. A No. 2 sable brush is used to block in some of the darker areas of the face with a mixture of Indian red, yellow ochre, and cobalt blue. The hair is mainly yellow ochre with touches of violet, Indian red, and cobalt.

4 The stripes of the blanket are painted in slightly bolder colors. This provides the artist with a guide to the strength of tones to be used elsewhere in the portrait. The artist uses a No. 2 sable brush throughout the work, painting lines and tiny details with the tip of the bristles. Most of the color is applied "dry-into-dry," with each layer of wash being allowed to dry before more color is laid on.

THE EYES

The artist uses a mechanical leadholder to draw the outline of the eyes. This is done carefully, with special attention to the structure of the eye socket and the underlying eyeball. Working from light to dark, the artist uses a fine brush to paint the narrow shadow thrown by the eyelid across the eyeball.

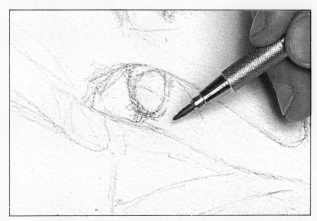

5 Using a mixture of violet, Payne's gray, and a touch of Indian red, the artist picks out the darkest shadows of the hair. These are a similar color to the cool shaded area of the face and blouse.

Against a Striped blanket.

6 The main areas of color and tone are now complete. The artist feels that the image is rather weak, lacking solidity and tonal interest. To complete the painting, she strengthens the flesh tones and darkens the clothing. The hair is worked into with a wider range of cool and warm colors, defining the curls and bringing out the texture of the hair.

Skin tones

The colors used here are alizarin crimson, lemon yellow, and tiny amounts of ultramarine and raw sienna. But the artist doesn't mix his colors together on the palette, since this would make them go flat and lifeless. Instead, he partly mixes them on the paper with small brushstrokes, layer upon layer.

Warm and cool colors

The skin appears lighter and warmer in the prominent, light-struck areas and darker and cooler in the receding or shadowed parts. Because warm colors appear to advance and cool colors to recede, you can use warm-cool color contrasts to model the "hills and valleys" of the face, much as sculptor pushes and pulls his block of clay. In *Portrait of Gaye*, notice the

subtle hints of cool blue and violet in the shadow of the side of the nose and under the lower lip, and the warm yellows on the forehead and cheek.

Luminosity

In a watercolor portrait, light reflecting off the white paper plays a vital role in creating an impression of the skin's

natural luminosity, so try to keep your colors as clear and fresh as possible. Following Paul Osborne's example, practice modeling the form of the face with small strokes of color, glazing thin layers over each other. Work on just-damp paper so that you can blend strokes wet-in-wet in the soft areas such as the cheeks.

▲ For pale skin tones the artist mixes alizarin crimson and lemon yellow, adding a touch of ultramarine for the cool shadow areas.

▲ For dark skin tones, use the same colors but add a touch of raw sienna or Hooker's green.

Portrait of Gaye by Paul Osborne.

SITTING CROSS-LEGGED

"Wet-into-dry" is the term used for the technique employed in this portrayal of a young person sitting cross-legged on a kitchen chair. It describes the process of applying a color wash over a dry color, as opposed to "wet-into-wet," when the colors are allowed to bleed into each other. Because the artist was painting with a lot of wet color, he used a hair drier in between stages to speed up the process.

The artist began with a pencil drawing which indicated the outlines and tonal areas of the subject. He worked into the drawing with the pale flesh tones of the face and hands, using pale washes in a base color of orange, alizarin, burnt umber, and yellow ochre. When these were dry the darker tones of the T-shirt were added, followed by the midle-tones of the hair in a darker version of the flesh color. As the shadows built up in an increasing variety of tones, the image began to emerge as a solid, recognizable form.

In a slightly unusual approach, the artist filled in the background after the subject was complete. He used the dark color of the background to define and develop the contours of the figure. For example, a small sable brush was used to pick out the spiky form of the hair and bangs, leaving narrow slivers of white paper as the highlights on the hair. In this way, the darkness of the background was actually used as a definitive outline for the central image.

The lettering on the shirt is important in this portrait because it describes the folds and creases and helps to give an impression of the form beneath. Here the artist worked directly by eye, in paint, using his experience to obtain an accurate rendering. Generally it would be necessary to draw the letters in pencil first before committing them to paint.

A sheet of stretched Bockingford watercolor paper was the support for this young boy's portrait. Standard sizes were unsuitable because the artist needed to work on a slightly narrower rectangle to accommodate the seated figure. He therefore cut the paper to meet his own requirements.

The lettering on the T-shirt and some of the deep clothing shadows were strengthened with the addition of gum water. A preliminary drawing was made with an F pencil, and the artist used a hair drier to speed up the drying process between stages.

2

1

1 The strong directional light on the seated child provides the artist with ample opportunity to use the classical watercolor technique of allowing the white paper to represent highlights.

2 The artist makes a light pencil drawing and starts to apply pale washes of color. Flesh tones are mixed from cadmium orange, alizarin crimson, burnt umber, and yellow ochre; shadows on the clothing are blocked in with cobalt blue, Payne's gray, and ivory black.

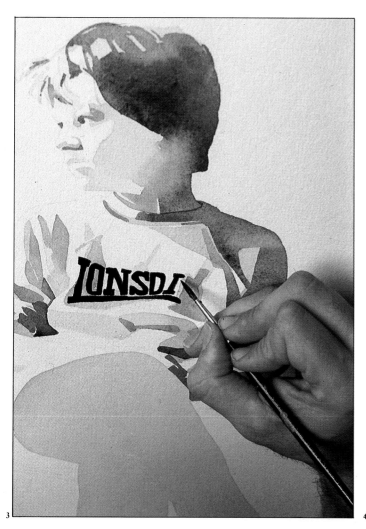

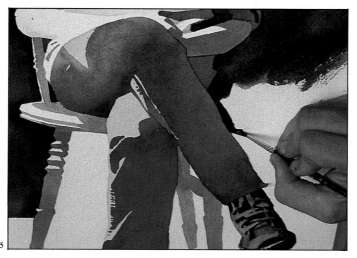

3 A darker flesh color is used for the middle tones of the hair. Shadows are added in raw umber and Payne's gray. Here the artist touches in the lettering on the T-shirt in pure black mixed with gum water.

4 The artist works across the image, strengthening the tones to develop the form. A mixture of black and Payne's gray is used to darken the clothing tones on the shaded side of the subject.

5 When the basic tones have been established, the background is blocked in with Payne's gray mixed with a little black. Using a No. 2 sable brush to take the paint up to the subject, the artist takes this opportunity to redefine and sharpen the outline of the figure.

Using the background to define shapes

The "negative space" of the background often provides the artist with a good opportunity to redraw and re-define the shape of the subject. Here the artist uses a small brush to take the background color up to the edge of the subject, at the same time tightening up and improving the contours of the boy's face and the line of the leg. Although this method is useful for making small alterations, it is a mistake to attempt any significant changes at this stage.

6

7

6 The imposition of the strong, dark background causes some of the figure tones to look weak and faded by comparison. To remedy this, the artist strengthens certain of the darkest shadows. For example, the eye and nostril have been picked out with a dense mixture of ivory black and burnt sienna.

7 Lettering on the T-shirt is painted accurately, the shape of the words being dictated by the folds and creases in the fabric. Gum water is mixed with the black paint to create a rich, dense tone — it also causes the paint to dry with a slight sheen. Both gum water and the thicker gum arabic can be used to enliven the normally matte finish of watercolor.

Sitting Cross-legged

MOUTHS

A smiling mouth is more difficult to paint than a mouth in repose, since any undue exaggeration of the smile results in a caricature rather than a portrait. The essential thing to remember is that we smile not only with our mouths but with our entire faces. Cover up the mouth in this portrait and you will see that the girl is still smiling. This is valuable proof that all the features of the head are interlinked and supportive of one another.

Obviously it would be difficult for a sitter to hold a smiling pose for a long period without the smile becoming somewhat "fixed." In this case, it might be helpful to take snapshots of your sitter and use these as reference during the painting of the portrait.

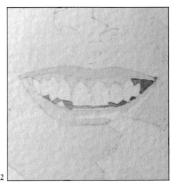

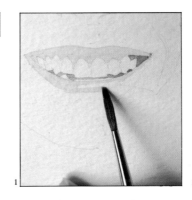

1 In this sequence, the artist demonstrates how he uses simple watercolor washes to render the important shadow patterns formed by the creases around a smiling mouth. After sketching in light pencil lines to establish the facial features and main shadow patterns, the artist begins painting the mouth. The dark line between the upper and lower teeth is painted with a light wash of ivory black, using the tip of a No. 2 sable brush. Then the upper gums are painted with a delicate tone of brown madder alizarin and cadmium orange. The same color is used on the lips, except for a small section of untouched paper on the lower lip which serves as a highlight.

2 When the first washes have dried, the artist blocks in the lightest tones around the mouth with a delicate wash of cadmium orange. A large area of white paper is left to indicate the light-struck area on the left side of the chin.

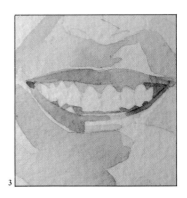

3 Next, the darker tones of the upper lip and the right side of the lower lip are painted with brown madder alizarin. When the light skin tone around the mouth has dried, the artist indicates the middle-toned shadow shapes with cadmium orange and a touch of burnt sienna. Already we can see the smile beginning to form.

4

4 When the middle tones are completely dry, the artist continues to build up the darker shadows by glazing with a mixture of cadmium orange and burnt sienna. The darkest shadows – under the nose and in the cleft of the chin – are painted with a mixture of burnt sienna and Payne's gray. It is important that each layer of color be perfectly dry before the next one is applied, so that the shadows remain clear and luminous.

5

5 The color on the shadow side of the face is darker, with further washes which accentuate the light-struck planes of the left side of the face. Finally a light mix of ivory black and yellow ochre is brushed onto most of the upper teeth, leaving one or two white highlights. This is another important point about painting mouths – always make teeth slightly darker in tone.

Hair

The average head contains around 100,000 separate hairs, but as far as the artist is concerned, hair should be rendered as one solid form, with planes of light and shadow. The volume of the head is defined by the hair, so it is important to begin by defining the hair in terms of shape and mass before thinking about texture. Search out those areas that catch the light and those that are in shadow, and indicate them with broad washes of color. Having established the underlying form, indicate the direction of the hair growth: long, flowing strokes for long hair, short, scumbled strokes for curly hair. Again, think in terms of mass — don't paint individual strands that seem unconnected to the rest of the hair.

To portray the essentially soft, pliant nature of hair, it is best to work wet-in-wet, so that the edges between the hair and the face, and the hair and the background, flow into one another. One of the commonest errors made by beginners is to make the hairline too hard. The hair and face should flow together as one entity; this is achieved by running some of the skin color into the hairline to soften the division between hair and face. Similarly, the outer edge of the hair should melt into the background color: soft edges here will give an impression of air and atmosphere around the sitter.

The color of hair should also look soft and natural, and should not attract attention away from the face. Even if your sitter has raven black hair, do not paint it black. Hair picks up reflected color from its surroundings: look for subtle hints of blue and brown in black hair, blonde and red in brown hair, and brown, gold, and gray in blonde hair.

TROUBLE-SHOOTING

Figure painting in watercolor has a reputation for being difficult, if not downright impossible. But, as so often happens in watercolor, the biggest difficulties usually arise from the artist's lack of confidence and an unwillingness to let go and allow the medium its fullest expression.

The portrait on the right is a case in point. The student's lack of confidence is betrayed by the stiff and awkward rendering of the figure, with its rigid pose and tightly drawn outlines. It is an understandable mistake to "clam up" when faced with a difficult subject; but it's a mistake that's death to any watercolor.

The answer is to learn to enjoy the fluid and mercurial qualities of watercolor — qualities that make it ideal for depicting the subtle lines and curves of the human form and the play of light upon its surfaces. The best watercolor portraits are not "posed" at all but are painted on the spur of the moment, perhaps when the subject happens to be relaxing in an armchair or strolling in the garden. *9:30am* by Joan Heston, on the opposite page, is a delightful example of a relaxed and informal portrait, with none of the stiffness that can result when a sitter is forced into holding a static and unnatural pose for a long period of time.

No boundaries

One habit that should be dropped like a hot potato is that of drawing a rigid outline of the figure and filling it in with color. This kills any feeling of life and movement in the figure and effectively cuts it off from the background so that it looks like a cardboard cut-out. By all means, make a few light pencil marks to plot the position of the figure, but don't treat them as boundary lines that cannot be crossed; nothing should be allowed to inhibit the speed and flow of your washes.

Notice in *9:30am* how the outlines of the figures are mainly soft-edged and blend naturally into the surrounding space. This gives an impression of a living, breathing person: we feel that the woman could get up out of her chair at any moment. However static the pose may be, you can still give the image fluidity.

In this disappointing portrait, the sitter looks more like a doll than a human being.

Keep it fluid

If you work in a dry and sparing manner, with timid brushstrokes and a brush that is starved of paint, it's not surprising if the finished result looks lifeless. Always use as large a brush as you dare, to discourage fiddly strokes, and load it with plenty of pigment. It's a good idea to work on damp paper; this makes it easier to lift out color for highlights, or to wipe out mistakes. It also means that your colors can flood into each other, creating subtle, translucent skin tones.

9.30am by Joan Heston.

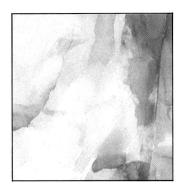

◄◄ The crisp edge of bare paper suggests strong sunlight lighting up the edge of the face. Bold, overlaid washes in the face add a lively touch.

◄ "Lost" edges help to unite the subject with the surrounding space.

· CHAPTER FOUR ·

Flowers

INTRODUCTION

Flowers, with their rich and varied array of glowing colors, their intricate forms and delicate structures, are an irresistible subject for painters. What is more, unlike the human and animal world, they do remain still for long enough to be painted. There are many different pictorial approaches to this branch of painting, all eminently suited to the medium of watercolor. Flowers can be painted in their natural habitats or indoors as still life arrangements; they can be treated singly or in mixed groups; they can be painted in fine detail or broadly and impressionistically.

Flower painting in history

Today flower paintings are hugely popular and avidly collected, and good flower painters can command high prices for their work. This is a relatively recent trend in terms of art history, however. In the Medieval and Renaissance periods, when scientists were busily cataloguing herbs and plants, the main reason for drawing and painting them was to convey information, and a host of illustrated books, called herbals, began to appear, explaining the medicinal properties of various plants and flowers. Many of the drawings were crude and inaccurate, but there were notable exceptions where the illustrators seemed to have worked from life, and these were the forerunners in a continuing and still flourishing tradition of botanical illustration.

The concept of painting flowers for their own sake owes more to the Flemish and Dutch still-life schools than to any other. The Netherlandish artists had always been more interested in realism and the accurate rendering of everyday subjects than their Italian and French counterparts, and throughout the sixteenth, seventeenth, and eighteenth centuries, they vied with one another to produce ever more elaborate flower pieces, with every petal described in minute detail. Artists have been painting flowers ever since, and although

critics in France formerly regarded flower pieces and still life as inferior art forms, even there they had become respectable by the mid-nineteenth century.

Working methods

Because flowers are so intricate and complex, there is always a temptation, whether you are painting them indoors or in the garden, to describe every single petal, bud, and leaf in minute detail. In some cases there is nothing wrong with this (for anyone intending to make botanical studies it is the only possible approach), but too much detail in an arranged flower piece or an outdoor painting can look unnatural and static, and there is also the ever-present danger of overworking the paint and losing the clarity of the colors.

Before you start a painting, make some hard decisions about which particular qualities you are most interested in. If you are inspired by the glowing mixture of colors in a summer flower-bed, treat the subject broadly, perhaps starting by working wet-in-wet, adding crisper definition in places so that you have a combination of hard and soft edges.

Always remember that flowers are living things, fragile and delicate, so don't kill them off in your painting — try to suit the medium to the subject. You can make a fairly detailed study, while still retaining a sense of freedom and movement, by using the line and wash technique, combining drawn lines (pen or pencil) with fluid washes. Never allow the line to dominate the color, however, because if you get carried away and start to outline every petal you will destroy the effect. Liquid mask can be helpful if you want to be able to work freely around small highlights, and attractive effects can be created by the wax resist method.

Finally, even a badly overworked watercolor can often be saved by turning it into a mixed-media painting, so before committing hours of work to the wastepaper basket, consider using pastel, acrylic, or opaque gouache on top of the watercolor.

Red Roses in a Flowerbed by Audrey Macleod.

One of Macleod's primary concerns, whether she is painting flowers or portraits, is the overall design of her paintings. Here she has used the different characteristics of the plants to create a strong pattern in which soft, round shapes are contrasted with spikier, more angular ones. Parts of the paper have been left bare to stand as highlights, but the tiny clusters of leaves on the right have been lightly touched in with opaque paint.

COLOR BLEEDING

Watercolor uses transparency to create both color and tone. For this reason white is not normally a part of the watercolorist's palette and thus the artist must rely on the various techniques and color mixes to achieve a successful picture. In this painting the variety of techniques illustrate the flexibility of the medium, as well as the skill required to use it to its best potential. Needless to say, it is worthwhile experimenting with color bleeding until you achieve an acceptable result.

The demands of using watercolor require that the artist be able to anticipate what will happen in advance of putting the paint on the surface. This can be very much a hit or miss effort even for the most experienced watercolorist, especially when applying loose washes of color or letting colors bleed into one another. The artist has a certain amount of control over where and how the paint is applied, but once the brush touches the paper there is much that can happen that the artist will not be able to predict accurately.

In this case, although care was taken to capture a true representation of the subject, the background was described in a more or less *ad hoc* manner, allowing paint and water to mix and with no attempt to control its movement on the surface.

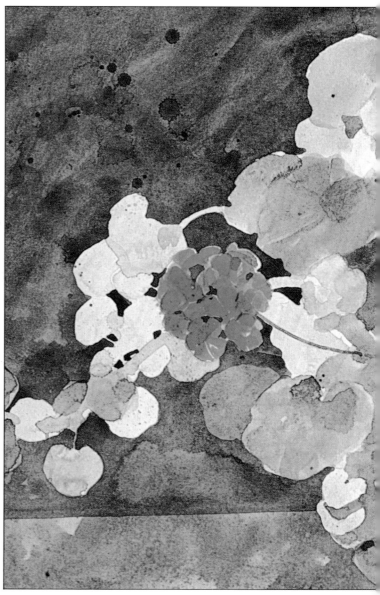

Pansies by David Hutton.

▲ To capture the velvety texture of these wine-dark pansies, the artist wetted the flower shapes with clear water and dropped his colors in when the paper had almost dried, allowing them to spread and mingle softly together.

1 Mix a very wet wash of cadmium green and water and loosely define the leaf shapes with a No. 6 brush.

2 With a small amount of cerulean blue and a No. 2 brush, put in the dark areas of the flowers. Mix green and yellow ochre, and lay in the dark areas of the leaves.

3 Mix a large, wet amount of Payne's gray, cerulean blue, and water. With a No. 10 brush, put in the background. Keep the paint very wet as you work.

4 With a No. 2 brush, develop dark tones of the leaves by mixing Payne's gray with green. Again, keep the mixture wet and let colors bleed into one another.

5 With a No. 2 brush, apply details of stems and veins in pure Payne's gray.

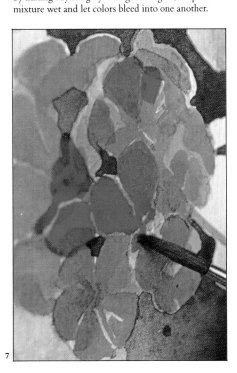

To bring the picture together and make it more interesting, in the final stages the artist concentrated on darkening and strengthening the overall image. The background was brought down to describe the foreground plane, and leaves and flowers were retouched with stronger tones.

6 With a very wet wash of water and green, the artist describes the general leaf shapes. The wet paint is pulled out of these areas in thin strands to create the stems of the leaves.

7 With a small sable brush the artist is here touching in areas of deep red over the lighter underpainting. From a distance, this will give the flowers depth and texture.

TONES

Use of light and tone is important in any painting, but has a special role in work on flowers, as these examples show. Careful observation and arrangement pay dividends, but do not be afraid to bring some spontaneity to your painting, too, especially when sketching to get an idea of how the tones work together.

Roses by Clarice Collings.

► Be spontaneous! Watercolor is the ideal medium for portraying the magnificent shapes and colors of flowers. Here the artist works without the "safety net" of a pencil outline, capturing the shape of each leaf and petal with just one or two strokes and lifting out the wet color here and there to create tonal variety. This spontaneous approach gives an impression of life and movement.

Sun seekers by Frank Nofer.

► Painting flowers has much to do with seeing tones as it has to do with color. Although these tulips are vividly colorful, it is the arrangement of light and dark tones that ultimately makes this painting so successful.

Winter Rose in a Lalique Vase by David Hutter.

►► The vibrant pinks and yellow-greens in this lovely, delicate painting owe much of their richness to the color of the background, which has been chosen with great care. A neutral but far from characterless gray-brown, it is dark enough to make the flowers and leaves stand out but not so dark that they look like paper cut-outs. The flowers themselves are carefully modeled, and the rose shows a considerable range of both tones and colors, from the pale pink highlights at the edges of the petals to the dark blue-red of the shadows.

Honeysuckle and Flowering Bramble in a Jar by Jacqueline Rizvi.

▼ In this closely-observed flower study the artist has paid as much attention to tones as to color and texture. In so doing, she has created an impression of light and space as well as accurately describing each flower and leaf.

COMPOSITION

A still life consisting of a single vase of flowers, or one in which a vase of flowers forms the main subject, can present special compositional problems — mainly that of how to arrange it on the painting surface without leaving too much dull and featureless space around it. The artists here have overcome this problem in differing ways.

Jug of Forsythia by Charles Inge.

▼ "Less is more" in Chinese painting, and this still life has a perfect simplicity and balance that owes much to the traditions of the Orient. The artist has moved the jug of forsythia away from the center of the paper, thus creating a dynamic visual tension between the subject and the surrounding white space. Yet the expanse of stark white paper also provides an important release, and balances the weight of the jug and flowers. Had the artist placed the subject in the center of the paper, much of the energy of the painting would have been lost.

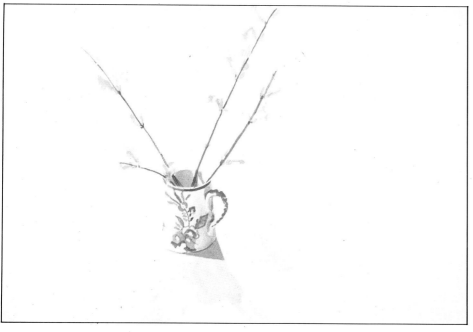

Lilies by Pamela Kay.

◀ Using a viewfinder can help you to frame your subject more imaginatively. In this painting, for example, the lilies are cropped off on the bottom and right, creating visual tension. Notice also how the artist has chosen a horizontal format, rather than a vertical one, for these tall flowers. You can almost feel the energy of the flowers thrusting diagonally upward to the top edge of the paper.

Snowdrops by Charles Inge.

▼ Background objects can introduce contrasting shapes and colors to your floral arrangements. In this painting the contrast is between the pureness and simplicity of the snowdrops and the complex decorative patterns on the jug and on the wallpaper. There's also an interesting juxtaposition between the curving shapes of the flowers and the bold diagonal shadow behind.

Hyacinths and Primroses by Pamela Kay.

◀ Too often, still lifes appear static and contrived, so it's refreshing to see a grouping like this one which has an easy naturalness about it. Spring flowers are ideally suited to informal arrangements. Here, the artist has massed together a collection of pots and vases of various size and shape, each filled with a wild tangle of hyacinths, primroses, and narcissi which create a riot of color.

TROUBLESHOOTING

So you've chosen your painting subject, which happens to be a vase of flowers. Now comes the moment of truth. You are confronted with an object and a sheet of pristine white paper: do you panic and dive straight into the painting, hoping it will turn out allright? Or do you plan your composition calmly and rationally, so as to get the maximum impact out of your subject?

All too often, compositional decisions are made without sufficient thought, and without exploring all the creative possibilities. This applies particularly when the subject is a simple one like a vase of flowers. The inexperienced artist will often go for the conventional approach and place the subject squarely in the center of the paper, surrounded by a plain background. Although there's nothing instrinsically wrong with this set-up, it doesn't always make for an interesting picture because it's too "safe."

However, floral still lifes offer you exciting opportunities for creating dynamic compositions. Don't limit yourself to approaches that are safe and comfortable: experiment with unusual viewpoints; try out different backgrounds; explore the potential of color interactions. It is the uniqueness of your point of view that will make people take notice of your pictures.

Frank Nofer's painting *Rhodies* on the opposite page has immediate visual impact. Note, for example, how the pale, delicate colours of the blooms are contrasted against a dark, dark background: a simple, effective device, yet one that many beginners would not think of using. Note also how the artist has included not just one vase of flowers but two, and how they are cleverly linked by the single, fallen bloom lying on the table. Remember, there's no reason why a floral still life has to consist of a single vase of flowers all on its own.

Be flexible

When planning a floral still life, never let your first compositional decision be your last. Try to see beyond mere "things" — a vase of flowers resting on a table, or whatever; look at your subject as a series of shapes, colors, and patterns that must link together harmoniously. These shapes, colors, and patterns are also the "words" with which you will speak to the viewer, so choose and arrange them carefully.

Flower paintings can lack interest.

Using a viewfinder

To help you visualize the different compositional options, examine your set-up through a cardboard viewfinder. First frame the overall composition. Does it look boring? Try moving in closer on one area. You may find that taking a small section from the subject will result in a more interesting composition.

Rhodies by Frank Nofer.

The pale blooms, linked by the flower on the table, draw the eye in a circular "pathway" through the painting.

Wet-in-wet mixtures of ultramarine, burnt sienna, and Winsor green are used to create richness and depth of color in the shadows and the dark background.

· CHAPTER FIVE ·

Landscapes and Buildings

INTRODUCTION

Whatever the medium used, landscape is among the most popular of all painting subjects, and among watercolorists, particularly amateurs, it ranks as the undisputed number one. One of the reasons for this is the common belief that it is easier than other subjects. Many who would never attempt a figure painting or flower study turn with relief to country scenes, feeling them to be less exacting and thus more enjoyable. This is perfectly understandable, and even quite a reasonable assumption; after all, it often does not matter too much if the shape of a mountain or tree is not a precise translation of reality. However, a painting will certainly be marred by poor composition or mishandled colors — these things always matter, whatever the subject.

The best landscapes are painted by artists who have chosen to paint the land because they love it, and use the full range of their skills to express their responses to it, not by those who see it as an easy option.

Direct observation

Another factor that separates the really good from the just-adequate is knowledge — not just of painting methods but of the subject itself. This is why most landscape painters work outdoors whenever they can. Sometimes they only make preliminary sketches, but often they will complete whole paintings on the spot. This, of course, is not always easy, but even if you only jot down some rapid color impressions, it is still the best way to get the feel of a landscape.

If you use photographs as a starting point — and many professional artists do take photos as a back-up to sketches — restrict yourself to a part of the countryside you know well and have perhaps walked through at different times of the year so that you have absorbed its atmosphere. Nature's effects are transient and cannot be captured adequately by the camera, so if you try to copy a photograph of a scene you are not familiar with, your painting is likely to have the same frozen-in-time look as the photograph.

Composition

Nor should you attempt to copy nature itself: painting is about finding pictorial equivalents for the real world, not reproducing it in precise detail. This means that you have to make choices and decide how much to put in or leave out and think about whether you might usefully exaggerate a certain feature in the interests of art. For instance you might emphasize the feeling of space in a wide expanse of countryside by putting in some small figures in the middle distance, or convey the impression of misty light by suppressing detail and treating the whole scene in broad washes.

The medium

Watercolor seems to be almost tailor-made for landscape painting, as its fluidity and translucency are perfectly suited to creating impressions of light and atmosphere. Light and portable, it has always been popular for outdoor work, but until you have gained some practice, it can be tricky to handle as a sketching medium. There is always the temptation to make changes in order to keep up with the changing light, and if there is too much overworking, the colors lose their freshness, defeating the aim of the exercise. There are ways of dealing with this, however. One is to work on a small scale, using the paint with the minimum of water so that you cut down the time spent waiting for each layer to dry, and another is to work rapidly wet-in-wet, concentrating on putting down impressions rather than literal descriptions.

If watercolor proves too frustrating, you may find gouache a good substitute. It can be used thinly, just like watercolor, but dries much more quickly and can be built up in opaque layers for the later stages.

If you intend to complete a whole painting on location rather than just making sketches, it is a good idea, if the subject is at all complex, to make the preparatory drawing the day before. Once the foundation is laid, you can approach the painting with confidence the following day. The chapter opens with advice on landscapes, and later we will look at techniques for painting buildings.

Tall Tree and Buildings by Charles
Knight RWS, ROI.

Knight's atmospheric landscapes are
marked by the economy with which he
describes his shapes, forms, and textures
— he never uses two brushstrokes when
one will suffice. Here he has painted
freely but decisively in a combination of
wet-in-wet, wet-on-dry, and dry brush,
leaving little specks of the paper showing
through the paint in places to hint at
texture.

SAND

The texture of sand, whether on beaches or in the desert, should be treated as simply as possible.

Start by indicating the patterns of light and shade on the sand, using warm and cool colors and working in broad washes of thin paint. In the foreground, use drybrush or spatter to suggest the granular texture of the sand and any small stones or pebbles. In watercolor, this texture is suggested most efficiently by using colors that separate, or granulate, on the paper; try using cerulean or manganese blue with a touch of burnt sienna for the shadows.

The colors of sand vary enormously from one part of the world to another, so there are no hard and fast rules about color mixtures. In general, though, sand is not as yellow as beginners often paint it. It is usually a pale yellow-gray in hue, particularly in the shadowed parts of sand dunes.

3 This picture shows how the spattered color has dried to a subtle tint which looks entirely natural.

4 When the first layer of spatter is completely dry the artist moves the paper mask down a few inches and spatters again, this time using a slightly darker tone with more Payne's gray added to it. When the mask is removed, the spattered area has a gradated appearance which strenghens the sense of perspective.

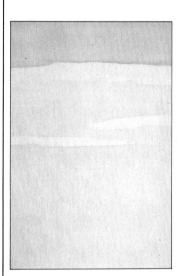

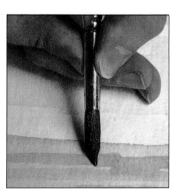

1 The artist begins by applying the first underwashes of color to define the areas of sand and water. Starting at the top of the paper, he lays a flat wash of cobalt blue for the water. Leaving narrow areas of white paper (which will later indicate ripples in the water), he then applies a dilute wash of yellow ochre and ivory black in the middle ground, to imply wet sand. This wash is warmed with more yellow ochre in the immediate foreground. The gradation from warm yellow in the foreground to cool blue in the background creates a sense of deep space.

2 When the first washes are dry, the artist begins texturing the rough sand in the foreground. He carefully masks off the rest of the painting with a large sheet of paper, then spatters a dilute mixture of yellow ochre and Payne's gray across the bottom third of the picture. This is done by running a finger through the bristles of a stenciling brush held several inches above the surface.

5 When the spattering is completed, the artist paints the large pebbles in the foreground. He uses a dark but fluid mixture of ivory black and a touch of yellow ochre, applied with a No. 10 sable brush, and varies the density of color to give tonal variation among the pebbles.

6 Finally, the ripples in the water are indicated by brushing in darker strokes of cobalt blue over the initial wash.

7 In the completed painting you can see how these simple techniques combine very effectively to create a convincing impression of a sandy beach. Notice how the texture of the pebbles in the foreground is created in a delightfully accidental fashion: the transparency of the paint used for the pebbles allows the spattered underlayer to show through, creating a suitably mottled texture.

Sand dunes

When painting sand dunes, what you leave out of the picture is as important as what you put in: use understated color and a minimum of brushstrokes to capture their pale, silvery tones and softly curving forms. In this watercolor painting, the white of the paper does much of the work in conveying the bleaching effect of bright sunlight on the sand.

1 After making an initial pencil outline of the scene, the artist begins by painting the sea and sky area with a pale wash of cobalt blue, leaving a little white at the top of the sky to indicate clouds. Then the lightest tones (apart from white) in the sand are brushed in, using a mixture of yellow ochre and lemon yellow. Next the middle tones are added, using the same mixture but with a touch of Payne's gray added to darken it. Finally the curves of the dunes are strengthened with more shadows, this time darkened still further with a touch of burnt sienna.

2 When the painting is dry, a very light spatter is applied in the immediate foreground to give a granular texture to the sand. The beach grasses are painted next, using dark mixtures of Hooker's green and burnt sienna, applied with short, scrubby brushstrokes. These accents of vivid green make a perfect foil for the pale, delicate tones of the sand.

Finally, a few blades of beach grass sticking up through the sand are suggested by slender drybrush strokes made with the brush tip.

In the completed painting, notice how the hollows in the sand dunes have sharp edges which become softer as they move out into the light: this is what gives the sand its soft, sculpted appearance.

A GLASTONBURY ROMANCE

A broad sweep of landscape has an almost universal appeal. Most of us will go out of our way to enjoy a good view. City dwellers often find particular exhilaration in looking at wide open spaces and valleys such as the scene the artist has portrayed here. The complete absence of detail in the immediate foreground implies similar open spaces in the directions we cannot see, behind and to either side, as though we were alone in rolling countryside. All signs of human activity have been excluded from view, the scale of the valley and surrounding hills being given by the relative sizes of the trees as they diminish toward the distance. The considerable recession is achieved by using the very palest of colors for the hills on the horizon, with an alternation of warm and cool to take our eye back across the valley. It is a romantic view of nature, in the tradition of many English watercolorists.

1

3

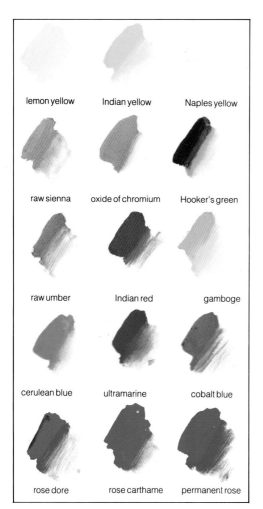

lemon yellow   Indian yellow   Naples yellow

raw sienna   oxide of chromium   Hooker's green

raw umber   Indian red   gamboge

cerulean blue   ultramarine   cobalt blue

rose dore   rose carthame   permanent rose

1 This painting demonstrates the classic watercolor technique of building from light to dark using thin washes of color.

2 Heavy white paper is used as the support, stretched on a board so that it continues to dry flat as successive layers of wet paint are applied.

3 The texture is varied by using various shapes and sizes of brushes and by working wet into wet, as here, or by laying fresh color over dried paint.

4 The combination of wet washes of color and small shapes that provide detail must be carefully controlled, as watercolor stains the paper and is not easily corrected. The choice of brush is important at each stage, and a preference will soon be found. A round sable or pointed Chinese brush is preferable for details.

5 A wide bristle brush is more suitable for laying in heavy washes.

Watercolors are best mixed in a plastic or ceramic dish, which must be white so that the strength of the color can be seen. Because the colors lighten on drying, the washes should be more intense than may appear necessary. This is a matter of judgment which develops with practice.

1
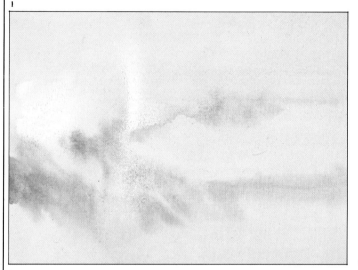

2

4

3

1 Broad areas of color are laid to define different elements of land and sky. Here a central division of the picture plane is made with a line of green over a basic wash of cerulean blue, raw umber, and indigo. The color is laid very thinly. Wet colors are brushed into the wash and allowed to spread on either side of the line, giving the rough shape of the valley.

2 As the paint dries the areas are given more emphasis, making use of the fuzziness of spreading colors and the tunnels forming on the paper in which heavier tones collect.

3 As the basic forms of the valleys emerge, small dabs and strokes of raw umber, ultramarine, and a mixture of the two are put in to show the lines of trees and hedges in the middle ground.

4 One dramatic sweep of a large bristle brush well loaded with a mixture of Hooker's green and raw sienna fills the foreground. The previous washes should be nearly dry so the line between the fore- and the middle ground should be well defined, with a fairly wide edge.

This largely alters the character of the work and gives a strong tone against which the other details can be emphasized. The horizon and sky are given a lighter tone by lifting paint with clean water and a sponge or dry brush.

5 Heavy tonal details are added to strengthen the hills in the middle distance on either side, and a line of dark trees is put in to define the recession in the foreground. If the painting is allowed to dry, the true tonal relationships can be seen and adjusted as necessary in the final stage.

Backruns

There is no remedy for a backrun except to wash off the entire area and start again. However, many watercolor painters use them quite deliberately, both in large areas such as skies or water and in small ones such as the petals of flowers, for the effects they create are quite unlike those achieved by conventional brushwork. For example, a realistic approximation of reflections in gently moving water can be achieved by lightly working wet color or clear water into a still damp wash. The paint or water will flow outward, giving an area of soft color with the irregular, jagged outlines so typical of reflections. It takes a little practice to be able to judge exactly how wet or dry the first wash should be, but as a guide, if there is still a sheen on it, it is too wet and the colors will merge together without a backrun, as they do in the wet-in-wet technique. These are both a nuisance and a delight to watercolor painters. If you lay a wash and apply more color into it before it is completely dry, the chances are that the new paint will seep into the old, creating strangely shaped blotches with hard, jagged edges — sometimes alternatively described as "cauliflowers." It does not always happen: the more absorbent or rough-textured papers are less conducive to backruns than the smoother, highly sized ones, and with practice it is possible to avoid them altogether.

Here backruns have been deliberately induced and then blown with a hair drier so that they form definite patterns. Techniques such as this are particularly useful for amorphous shapes such as clouds, reflections, or distant hills.

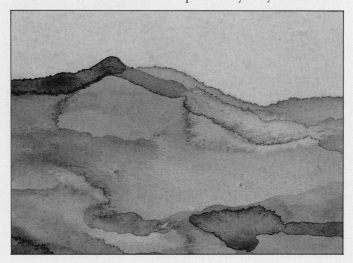

IRISH HILLS

Watercolor is a medium that is ideal for achieving very soft and gradual changes of tone and color combined with a direct and spontaneous technique. Consequently, it is well suited to representing changing weather conditions, when clouds alter from one moment to the next; above all, it is very suitable for rendering the watery skies of northern Europe. This painting exploits the appropriateness of the medium for the subject, evoking those days when dark rain clouds alternate with sudden and brief bursts of sunshine. It also shows the effectiveness of using a large brush loaded with water. This technique produces unique drying marks, wholly consistent with the nature of the subject, when the water is absorbed by the paper.

The artist has made the weather and its effect on the landscape the main theme here, allowing the merging of sky and hills to fuse mysteriously. The pictorial space is created to some extent by the decreasing size of trees and fields, but more by atmospheric perspective, with warm colors in the foreground receding to cool blues and grays in the distance.

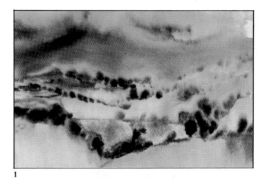

1

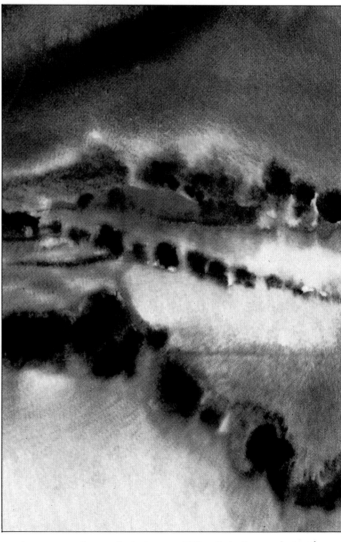

2

lemon yellow	Indian yellow	Naples yellow
raw sienna	oxide of chromium	Hooker's green
raw umber	Indian red	gamboge
cerulean blue	ultramarine	cobalt blue
rose dore	rose carthame	permanent rose

1 A sharp contrast of tone and color is conveyed through a technique in which the blurring and soft interaction of wet watercolor washes suggest the forms.

2 The painting is atmospheric rather than fully descriptive and is created on a small scale which gives a certain vigor and tension to the marks.

3

4

Using gouache for landscapes

Gouache paints dry very quickly – which makes them ideal for rapid painting on the spot. Look at *Olive Trees near Rhonda* by Jeremy Galton. Most of the colors in this painting have been mixed with quite a lot of white, producing a high-key picture compatible with the dazzling light of southern Spain. The distant mountains have been lightly glazed over with white paint, used sufficiently thinly for the colors beneath to show through, a technique commoner in acrylic than in gouache.

Olive Trees near Rhonda by Jeremy Galton.

3 A soft Chinese brush which has a thick base of hairs tapering to a very fine point, is used. Details of the painting show how fluid brushstrokes encourage the natural flow of the watery paint.

4 Broad sweeps of color laid with a round, soft brush melt together and spread more readily if the paper is already dampened with clean water.

5 The color can be lightly controlled or lifted by dabbing gently with an absorbent sponge or pad of tissue. This alters the tone and texture of the paint and also speeds up the painting process by removing the excess moisture so colors can be overlaid more quickly.

6 A medium-sized sable brush is a good alternative to Chinese brushes for adding small details and precise shapes. It is vital to judge the drying time correctly so the color diffuses by just the right amount.

5

6

The painting has a well-defined color scheme, divided between the heavy blue of the mountain and the yellow tones in the foreground, linked by warm pink and gray washes and the dark lines of trees and bushes.

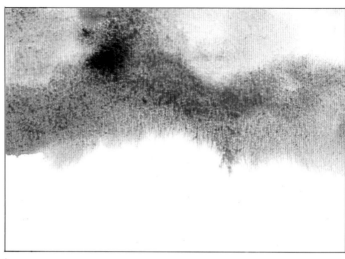

2

1

1 The dark band of blue is established immediately, merging gently into a wash of blue and rose, suggesting the sky.

2 These colors are put down with a lot of water so that the blue spreads and flows naturally, drying without harsh lines at each edge.

3 The mauve pink is extended into the foreground, and small patches of spring green and yellow are laid in, which follow the gently curving landscape below the mountain. The colors are mixed to form subtle grays, which shade and deepen the brighter hues. Well-judged control of the moisture is essential.

4 Details of the trees are developed with dark green and raw umber carefully placed in small dabs and patches. The tones are enriched and extended throughout the image.

5 Contrasts are built up more heavily in the final stage, with the colors brushed in and blotted to create form and space. To give a misty effect around the mountains and sky a little white is dropped into the color washes, making the paint slightly opaque.

5

Olive Trees near Ronda
by Jeremy Galton

Most of the colors in this painting have been mixed with quite a lot of white, producing a high-key picture compatible with the dazzling light of southern Spain. The distant mountains have been lightly glazed over with white paint used sufficiently thin for the colors beneath to show through, a technique commoner in acrylic than in gouache.

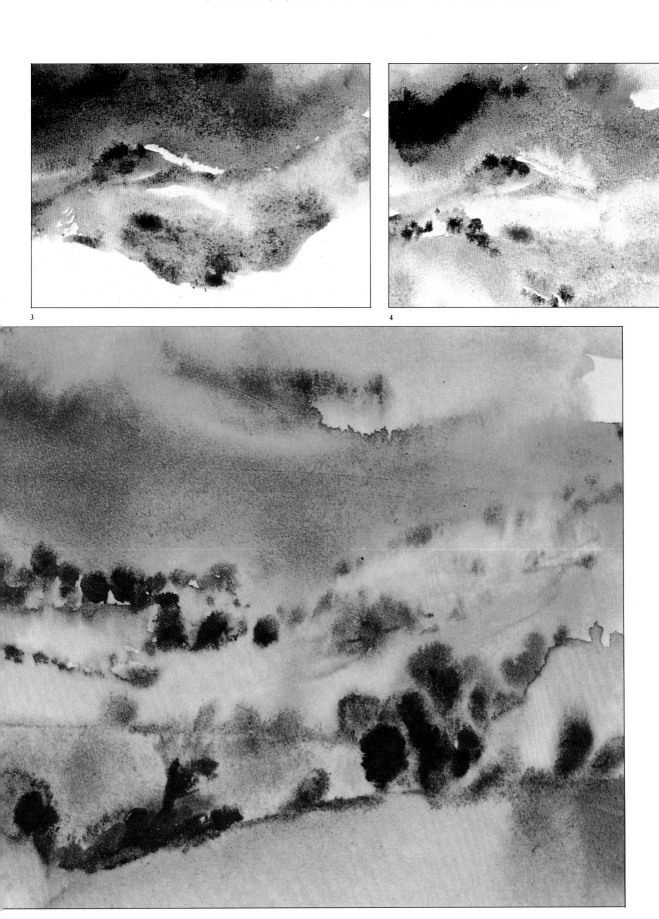

3

4

SUMMER PAINTING

In this work the artist was interested in the ways in which a landscape changes, sometimes dramatically, from season to season and under different weather conditions. Although the fields and hills are firmly established in space, it is not the artist's intention that we should see them separately from the low clouds that transform them. The transparency of watercolor has been used in varying degrees to achieve this.

The spontaneity which is so effective in this medium imposes considerable disciplines on the artist. To capture transitory cloud effects, in the manner we see here, involves working at great speed while judging the correct proportions of pigment and water, and getting it right the first time. There are some ways that mistakes can be rectified, but for pale and delicate passages, such as thin watery clouds, the work can quickly look labored and lack freshness if not applied swiftly and confidently.

Here the artist has observed the soft and subtle gradation of tone that give the scene its atmosphere.

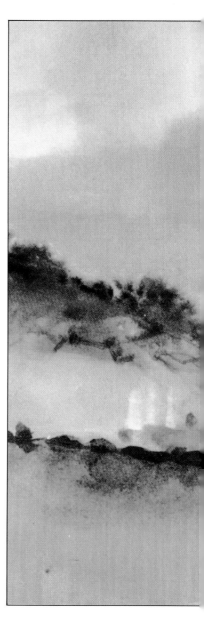

The work is laid flat (◄) to prevent the colors from running uncontrollably and to give free access to the painting. The brushwork should be loose and confident, giving a vigorous rhythm to the washes of color and lines of detail. As the tones gradually build up, the diffused colors form a web of shapes and hues which are drawn out by adding definition with the point of the brush (▲ right). Many colors are allowed to mix on the paper to achieve the full effect.

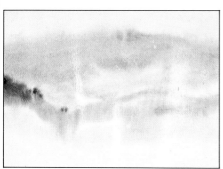

1 In the early stages the colors are deliberately allowed to blur and merge together, mixing into subtle tones which suggest the division between sky and land. The paper is wetted with clean water and blue, green, and yellow washes laid in, with a slightly darker emphasis added in raw umber on the left-hand side.

2 As the colors dry, a warm pink tone is brushed into the sky and touches of blue in the middle ground.

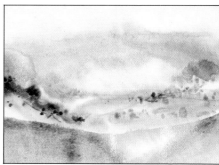

3 The foreground is blocked in with a broad-bristle brush, the paint still kept wet so that it dries in a mass of uneven tone. More detail is given to the middle ground with green and brown mixtures.

7

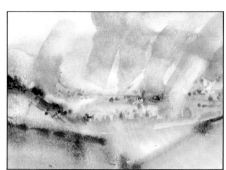

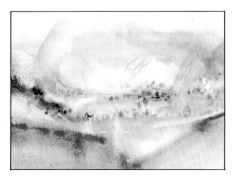

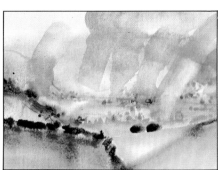

4 The sky is given a yellow cast to represent light breaking through the cloud, and this is overlaid with diagonal strokes of blue-gray.

5 These strokes are made more emphatic and merged into the blues in the landscape.

6 The foreground colors are strengthened.

7 Finally the stormy sky is given an opaque gray cast by adding a little white to the paint.

Capturing the effects of light

To capture the effects of light with brush and pigment is an extremely difficult task. Watercolor is the perfect medium for this task, as its rich translucent hues and subtle tonal mixtures have the delicacy necessary for effective rendering.

2

3

1 In this subject there is a combination of the brightness of summer light and the heavy atmosphere created in a passing shower.

2 Again the basic areas of color are built up in broad washes of thin paint.

3 Details are added with accurately placed patches of tone and color. As the landscape takes shape the brushstrokes become all-important, especially in the final stages where broad bands of gray are laid over the colors to create the atmospheric effect of rain clouds.

1

View from Hod Hill by Ronald Jesty ▶

The eye is always drawn to human figures in a landscape, and their inclusion can turn an ordinary subject into a striking picture. Here the two figures on the right, tiny as they are, form the anchoring point for the whole composition. We look first at them; then, following their gaze, we explore the rolling landscape beyond.

Venice: Punta della Salute
by J M W Turner

Many artists have a certain favorite theme or motif which appears frequently in their paintings. For the English artist Joseph Mallord William Turner (1775-1851), that theme was light. And it was the magical effects of the light of Venice which had the most profound effect on Turner's work.

CREATING EFFECTS

Watercolor is one of the most versatile of drawing media. It can be handled with precision for fine detail work but is also naturally suited to a fluid and spontaneous style. You can exploit random effects in the flow and fall of the paint by spattering color from the end of the brush or blowing the thin, wet washes into irregular rivulets across the paper. Integrate these marks with carefully controlled brushwork to vary the textures in the painting.

The full effect of watercolor depends upon luminous, transparent washes of color built up layer upon layer. As white paint deadens the freshness of color, small areas of highlight are achieved by leaving the white paper bare while light tones are produced by using thin washes of color. Dark tones are slowly brought to a suitable intensity by the use of several successive applications of thin layers of the same color.

The urn shape was initially protected with a layer of masking fluid, painted carefully into the outline. This seals off the paper while the rest of the surface is freely painted over with large brushes and watery paint. When the work is complete and dry you can then rub off the mask and work on shadows and highlights of the shape with a small brush.

1

2

3

4

5

6

1 Sketch in the basic lines of the drawing with a pencil, carefully outlining the shape of the urn. Paint in this shape with masking fluid and let it dry completely.

2 Use a No. 10 ox-eye brush to lay a broad light wash of cobalt blue across the top half of the painting and chrome green and Payne's grey across the foreground.

3 Mix a dark, neutral grey and paint wet streaks of color to form the trunks of the trees. Blow the wet paint in strands across the paper making a network of branches.

4 As the paint dries, work over the structure with green, grey and umber rolling the brush into the pools of paint and letting the color spread.

5 Load a decorators' brush with paint and flick tiny spots of color into the washes. Block in the shape of the wall with a thin layer of red and brown using a No. 6 brush.

6 Work over the foreground with the decorator's brush loaded with Hooker's green, using a rough, scrubbing motion. Draw in details on the wall.

7 Let the painting dry completely. Gently rub away the masking fluid with your finger — make sure all the fluid is off and try not to damage the paper.

8 Paint in the shadows on the urn in brown and grey, adding a little yellow ochre and light red to warm the tones. Paint the form and stonework.

7

8

Masking fluid, spattering, blotting and stippling

To create a spattered effect, load a large bristle brush with paint and quickly run your finger or a small knife through the hairs.

An alternative to spattering paint is to stipple with the end of a broad bristle brush. Here the artist is using a decorators' brush to lay in small dots of color.

A dense, leafy texture can be achieved by blotting a wet area with a piece of tissue. Do not rub but simply put the tissue down, press, and pick it up to leave the small gaps and crevices in the paint surface.

Masking fluid may be used to protect the white paper from the paint. When the painting is completed, rub off the fluid with your finger. If the fluid is put on with a brush, make sure to rinse the brush immediately after use.

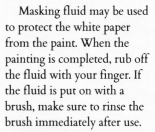

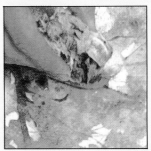

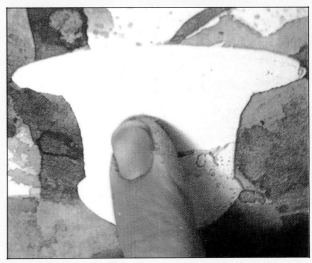

BUILDING THE IMAGE

The techniques required for this type of painting are quite lengthy, and it is advisable to practice on scraps of a similar paper before beginning the actual painting.

A large, wet pool of color will dry with a gradated tone and strong, irregular outline. Overlaying a succession of washes produces vivid colors, a patterned network of light and dark tones, and linear detail suggesting the texture of foliage and flowers. You can speed up the drying process with a hair drier or fan, but since this tends to deaden the color, it is best to let the painting dry naturally.

The image is built up in the traditional watercolor technique of working from light to dark. Start by laying in pale tones in thin, broad washes, leaving patches of white paper to form highlight areas. Because the paint is so fluid, only one good-quality, medium-sized sable brush is needed. Make broad sweeps of watery color with bristles loose or spread, and bring the tip to a point for finer details. Study each shape carefully, and draw directly with the brush. Color can be lifted from the surface with a clean, damp cotton swab to lighten the tones. Detailed corrections are difficult with this type of painting, but it is possible to make small corrections by rubbing the surface when completely dried with a fine-grained sandpaper.

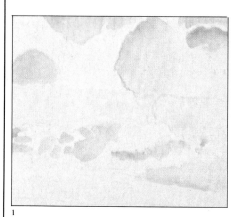

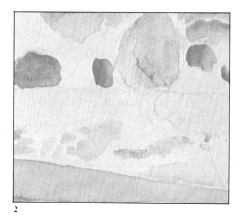

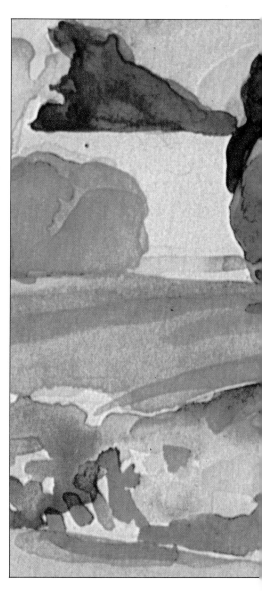

1 Sketch out the composition very lightly with an HB pencil. Lay washes of thin wet paint to establish basic forms and local colors.

2 Work over the painting again with light washes, blocking in more shapes. Let the colors run together in patches to create a soft, fuzzy texture.

3 Let the painting dry, and then apply layers of denser color, gradually building up the forms with thin overlays.

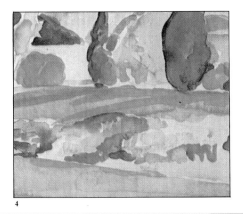

4 Paint in the shadow shapes over the grass with broad streaks of blue and green. Work into the trees with overlapping areas of color to show the form.

5 Strengthen dark tones in the background with Prussion blue and black. Lay a broad wash of yellow over the grass to lift the tone.

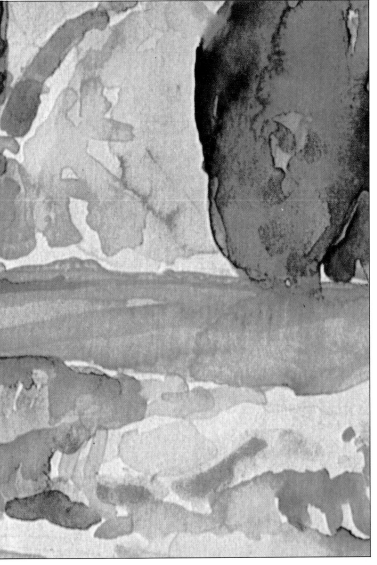

Cleaning with a knife, sanding and blotting

Where paint has inadvertently splashed on the white surface, the artist can very carefully scratch it off with a knife.

After scraping off spots or splashes, the artist is here very lightly sanding the surface with a fine-grade sandpaper. Use a very light touch.

To lighten a tone or stop the paint from bleeding, a cotton swab can be used to blot up excess moisture or color. This can also be used to blend colors.

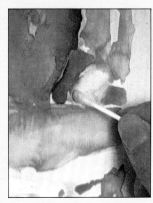

GETTING A PERSPECTIVE

The painting shown here captures a sense of distance by showing how the land recedes gradually from the foreground toward the horizon and by using the two trees as a central focus. This is achieved by carefully varying color tones — placing strong, warm hues in the foreground and colors that are cooler and less intense in the distance. The impression of receding space is enhanced by the sky gradually lightening and finally rising into a thin strip of white.

To keep an overall coherence to the picture, the colors in each area are subtly linked together. For example, the same blue has been used for the linear details in the middle distance, as in the shadow areas of the trees. A harmonious balance of warm and cool tones has been applied, as seen in the contrast between the warm brown of the foreground, the colder yellow across the center of the painting, and the reddish-brown and blue tones in the trees, which deepen the intensity of the green washes. The end result, seen on the opposite page, is a striking, dramatic, yet beautifully balanced picture.

1 First wet the paper using a large No. 8 brush dipped in water. Lay in a thin wash of Prussian blue with a No. 8 sable brush, working down from the top of the paper.

2 Brush in a yellow ochre wash across the center of the paper, leaving white space along the horizon line and in areas where the main forms will be placed.

3 Use viridian, emerald green, and burnt umber to apply the basic forms of the trees, indicating areas of light and shade.

4 Draw into the shapes of the trees in more detail with the point of a No. 6 brush. Darken the burnt umber with a little blue and mix yellow into the greens.

5 Continue to extend the forms and intensify the colors. Fan out the bristles of a No. 8 brush between thumb and forefinger to draw feathery texture.

6 Dampen the yellow ochre wash with clean water, and draw into it with a mixture of Payne's gray and blue.

7 Add detail into the gray area with ultramarine, keeping the paint thin and wet. Use the same blue in foliage shadows, and contrast with a warm reddish brown.

8 Mix up Payne's gray with burnt umber and lay a broad streak of color across the foreground with a No 8 sable brush, working directly onto the dry paper.

Dry-brush and the wash

A consistent, even wash can be achieved by mixing a large amount of paint and water in a small dish; dip a large sable brush into this, and move across the surface with an even pressure.

To effectively use the dry-brush technique, load a brush with paint, blot it on a rag, and grasping the brush hairs between the thumb and fingers, flick the brush on the surface to create a feathery texture.

TROUBLESHOOTING

In any landscape painting the foreground is often the trickiest part to handle. Include too much detail and you discourage the viewer's eye from moving back in the picture plane and exploring the rest of the composition. Put in too little detail, on the other hand, and the foreground becomes an empty, monotonous area.

The main problem with the painting on the right is the foreground fence. It is painted rather crudely and doesn't contain enough interesting color, texture, or light and shade to make it the focal point of the picture. Yet it is clumsy and obtrusive enough to set up a barrier between the viewer and the rest of the composition.

Foregrounds need to handled carefully. The trick is to be able to *suggest* detail and texture without overstatement, so that the viewer is aware that there are shadows on the grass, flowers in the field, or whatever, but does not have these details forced upon him or her. In other words, you have to mimic the way in which the human eye perceives things: when we focus on one particular object, the area around the object is seen more or less as a blur because the brain can only take in so much visual information at one time.

In *Farm House at Richmond* (opposite) artist Stan Perrott uses subtle modulations of color, texture, and tone to create a lively impression of the field in front of the house. These subtle details are pleasing to the eye, but they don't detract from the focal point of the picture, which is the group of farm buildings in the distance.

Tonal variety

If you have a large expanse of foreground, keep it lively by varying the tones and colors. This will encourage the viewer's eye to move around

The fence is rather obtrusive in this painting.

the picture space. In *Farm House at Richmond*, Stan Perrott painted the grass wet-in-wet and lifted off some of the paint with a damp natural sponge and blotting paper to create light areas.

Textural details

These can be suggested with dry brush strokes or picking out highlights with the blade of a sharp knife. Try spattering dark paint onto a light base wash to suggest stones and weeds, or spatter liquid mask onto a light base wash and then brush in a darker tone. Remove the mask, and *voilà!* you have light stones and weeds in a dark area.

Farm House at Richmond by Stan Perrott.

Light and dark greens keep the eye moving back in the picture plane, toward the focal point.

Drybrush and spattering techniques indicate weeds and grasses without looking too obtrusive. The white shapes of the daisies are preserved with liquid mask, which is removed when the painting is completed.

When spattering, dip a bristle brush or an old toothbrush into the paint, and draw your thumbnail quickly through the bristles to release a shower of fine dots onto the paper. Mask off the rest of the painting with newspaper — paint travels!

Use a damp brush, a piece of tissue, or a natural sponge to lift out pale areas in a dark wash and create tonal variety.

BUILDINGS

A lot of people steer clear of painting buildings because they feel they cannot draw well enough or are unable to come to grips with perspective. This is understandable, but it is a pity, as buildings not only form a major part of the twentieth-century landscape, but are also in many cases beautiful, exciting, and highly paintable.

Perspective and proportion

If you want to make detailed, accurate and highly finished paintings of complex architectural subjects, such as the great palaces and cathedrals of Europe, a knowledge of perspective is vital, as are sound drawing skills. This is a specialized kind of painting, but most people have humbler aims, and it is perfectly possible to produce a broad impression of such subjects or a convincing portrayal of a rural church, farmhouse, or street scene mainly by means of careful observation. Too much worrying about perspective can actually have a negative effect, causing you to overlook the far more interesting things, such as a building's general character, color, and texture. However, there is one important rule that most of us learn at school but don't pay much attention to, and this is that receding parallel lines meet at a vanishing point on the horizon. The horizon is at your own eye level, so is determined by the place you have chosen to paint from. If you are on a hill looking down on your subject, the horizon will be high and the parallels will slope up to it, but if you are sitting directly beneath a tall building, they will slope sharply down to a low horizon. It is vital to remember this when painting on the spot, because if you alter your position by, for example, sitting down, when you began the painting standing at an easel, the perspective will change, and this can be disconcerting.

If you intend to paint a "portrait" of a particular building, shape and proportion are just as important as they are in a portrait of a person — it is these that give a building its individuality. A common mistake is to misrepresent the size and shape of doors, windows, balconies, and so on in relation to the wall area, which not only makes it fail as a portrait but also creates a disturbing impression, as the building looks structurally impossible.

Before you start to draw or paint, look hard at the building and try to assess its particular qualities. Some houses are tall and thin with windows and doors occupying only a small part of each wall, while others seem to be dominated by their windows. In a street scene there may be several completely different types of building, built at various periods, and all with distinct characters of their own. You can exaggerate these for extra effect, but you ignore them at your peril.

Shapes and proportions can be checked by a simple measuring system. Hold a pencil or a small pocket ruler up in front of you, and slide your thumb up and down it to work out the height or width of a door or window in relation to those of the main wall. Most professional artists do this; the human eye is surprisingly untrustworthy when it comes to architecture.

The straight line problem

Unless you are a trained draftsman or just one of those lucky people, it can be extraordinarily hard to draw and paint straight lines, and a building that tilts to one side or that has outer walls that are not parallel to each other can ruin the impression of solidity as well as looking bizarre. The ruler is useful here too — there is nothing wrong with using mechanical aids for your preliminary drawing, as it will quickly be covered by the paint. You can apply colors as freely as you like once you have a good foundation, using the ruled lines as a general guide. Some nineteenth-century watercolorists were not above having their drawings done by professional draftsmen.

Studio View by Julia Gurney.

Paintings of buildings do not have to be minutely observed and correct in every detail. Here the artist has taken a broader approach, conveying the atmosphere of the city houses under a stormy sky through her bold and decisive use of mixed media. Detail is restricted to the foreground, which she has emphasized by picking out the pattern of the bricks and tiles.

VINEYARD IN ITALY

This painting is more a landscape than an architectural study. The buildings are just one of the features in a landscape, not the whole subject. They are treated quite sketchily, and their appeal lies in the way that the planes of the walls catch the light and the colors of the roofs balance the greens of the foliage. However, although not drawn in any great detail, the buildings are a large part of what the painting is about, and hence its focal point, and they have been treated with sufficient attention to perspective and proportion to insure that they look solid and convincing.

The painting was done on the spot, but the artist worked out his composition first by making a charcoal sketch, which clarified the subject for him and enabled him to see how best to treat it. He placed the group of houses slightly higher than they are in the sketch, so that almost no sky was visible, and altered the foreground so that the sweeping lines of the vineyard were made much stronger, leading the eye into the picture and up to the houses. This is a good example of the way an artist can ignore, emphasize, or alter any elements of the scene in front of him to make an interesting and lively composition. The busyness of the background, with the different shapes and colors of walls, roofs, and foliage, is accentuated by the strong, regular and linear pattern of the foreground, so that the whole painting has a sparkling air of movement. The use of complementary colors is also exemplary: the red of the roofs and the green of the foliage engage in a lively interplay.

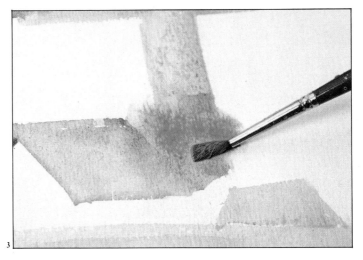

1 When painting on the spot, making a preliminary sketch is a good way to sort out your ideas before committing yourself to paint. It is essential to be sure of the most important elements of a landscape. Resist the temptation to put everything in just because it is there.

2 The artist's first step was to lay a neutral wash on the foreground area. This was a mixture of raw umber, Prussian blue, and permanent yellow. He then laid a second wash over it, using the same mixture, to create slight tonal differences and texture.

3 Having laid broad but precisely placed washes on the rooftops and shadowed sides of the buildings, the artist puts on an area of loosely applied bright green, thus juxtaposing complementary colors and establishing a key for the rest of the painting.

4 and **5**. Here the artist had to lay a wash against a complicated edge, the rooftops on the right-hand side of the picture. He first wet the paper only in the area to be covered, then worked paint into it, and finally dabbed it with blotting paper to absorb some of the excess paint, lighten the tone, and provide an even texture.

6 Here the artist is defining the shadows on the unlit sides of the buildings, allowing the paint to mix on the paper in order to produce a soft effect.

7 He uses a combination of Prussian blue and Payne's gray to achieve relatively strong tonal contrasts.

8 The paint was kept quite fluid throughout the painting, and the texture of the paper is an important element in the final effect. Here a large, soft brush is used to apply dark green over the light red of the roofs and the blue of the sky, so that the colors blend into one another in a pleasing way.

6

7

4

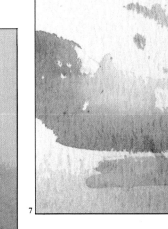

5

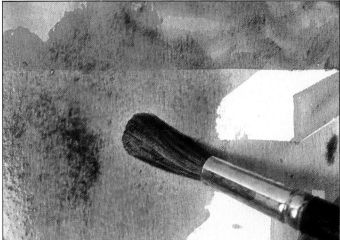

8

9

9 The lines of the vines are laid on with bold brush strokes and darkened in places to hint at shadow, without describing it in detail. Strong tonal contrasts help to bring the foreground forward toward the picture line.

10 The rows of vines are reinforced with a mixture of terre verte and Payne's gray. Shadows are not usually merely darker shades of the same color, but have their own colors.

10

CHURCH IN FRANCE

Buildings present special problems for the artist, especially the watercolorist, and they demand a fairly precise and planned method of approach. In a painting such as this, where the church is the *raison d'être* of the picture rather than being just one feature in a landscape, the perspective must be convincing, the lines sharp and clear, and some suggestion must be made of the texture of the masonry.

The artist has worked in a very deliberate way, starting with a careful outline drawing made with a sharp pencil and ruler to map out the main areas, so that he is sure where to place his first wash. He then put on a series of flat washes, the first one being laid over the sky area and the second, very pale, over the building itself. Next he began to consider the best way of suggesting the stonework, and decided on liquid mask, applied in slightly uneven brush strokes. When this was

dry he washed over the top with brownish gray paint and then removed the mask, leaving lines of paint between and around the original brush strokes. Further texture was applied at a later stage by the spattering method, and crisp lines were given to details, such as the face and hands of the clock, by drawing with a sharp pencil.

The whole painting has a pleasing crispness, produced by the very sharply defined areas of light and dark; no attempt has been made to blend the paint in the shadow areas, and very distinct tonal contrasts have been used — in the small round tree in front of the church, for example.

The artist has also avoided the temptation to put in too much detail, which might have reduced the impact and made the picture look fussy and untidy. The tiled roof consists simply of a flat wash; although there is just enough variation in the sky to avoid a mechanical look, no attempt has been made to paint actual clouds.

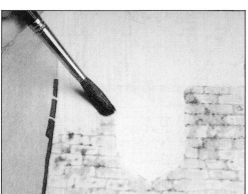

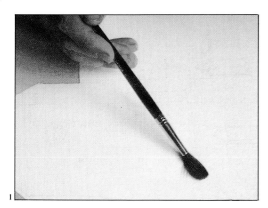

1 and **2.** In a subject like this a careful outline drawing is essential. Once the drawing was complete the artist laid an almost flat wash over the sky and then a paler one over the building. These established his basic middle-tones, enabling him to gauge the tonal strength of the steeple.

3 The steeple was painted and allowed to dry, after which liquid mask was put onto areas of the masonry, not as flat wash but as individual brush strokes. Fairly dark brownish paint was washed over this when dry so that it sank into the areas between the brush strokes.

4 Here the masking fluid is being rubbed off with a finger, leaving the irregular lines of dark paint to suggest the edges of the stones. This is a more effective method than painting in the lines, and gives a much more natural look because the technique is very slightly "random."

5 Here the spattering technique is being use to give further texture to the walls. It is sometimes necessary to mask off surrounding areas so that they do not get splashed, but this artist makes use of the method quite often, and is confident of his ability to control the paint.

6 At this stage only the foreground, with the dark trees and bright grass, remains unpainted. The artist worked the painting piece by piece; having no overlapping layers of paint gave a crisper definition, but this is not recommended for beginners, as it is difficult to judge tones and colors in isolation.

7 Here the hands and face of the clock are being carefully drawn in with a very sharp pencil over the original pale wash.

6

8

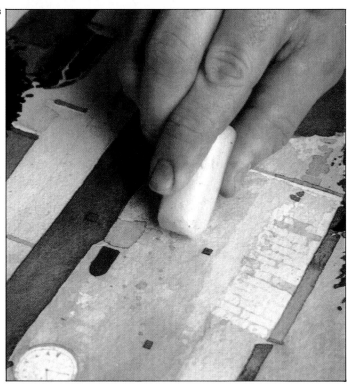

92

9

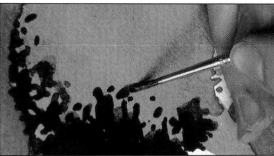

10

Church in France.

8 Further texture is given to the stonework by rubbing a candle over the paint. Candles or wax crayon can also be used as a resist method, like liquid mask, in which case they are applied before a final paint layer.

9 The middle-tones of the grass have now been laid in, providing a foil to the red-brown of the tiled roof.

10 The artist now works carefully on the shadow side of the tree, using a fine brush and very dense dark green paint.

11 The final touches were to darken the left-hand tree and paint in the straight, dark shadow in the foreground. Two small trees were also added in the shadow area at the bottom of the church.

Masking for buildings

Masking tape can be very helpful for buildings. It takes the tension out of painting, allowing you to work freely without the danger of spoiling an edge that needs to be straight and crisp.

TROUBLESHOOTING

A lot of beginners tend to shy away from painting buildings because they think an intricate knowledge of the rules of perspective is required. In the painting on the right, the student has cunningly avoided the problem of complicated perspective by painting the house from a straightforward viewpoint. The effect, however, is flat and one-dimensional, somewhat like a piece of stage scenery.

The subject appears to have been painted on a dull, overcast day: there are few contrasts of light and shade to emphasize form and bring out the interesting features and surface textures of this lovely old building. Note also the absence of a cast shadow to indicate that the archway and the portion of the upper story immediately above it project beyond the rest of the building. (By the same token, the shadow under the archway looks odd because it is the only really dark tone in the painting — it doesn't connect with anything.)

Another point to note is that the ends of the building are out of the picture, and this adds to the cardboard cut-out effect. The image would have been much stronger had the student moved the house farther back and set it against a contrasting background.

In *Delta Farm* by Stan Perrott (opposite) the building is not so grand as that in the problem painting, yet it looks far more solid and real.

Lighting

The form of an object is revealed by the contrast of light and shade on its surface, so shadows and cast shadows are a powerful element in making buildings look three-dimensional. Generally, late afternoon is a good time to paint buildings, when long shadows travel across the contours of walls and throw surface features into sharp relief. If possible, position yourself so that the sun is at a three-quarter angle to the building, because this the most revealing of form.

The building looks flat, like a cardboard cut-out.

In *Delta Farm*, note how the jutting gable on the farmhouse casts a strong diagonal shadow behind it. Without this shadow we would not know that this part of the building extends forward.

Lost and found edges

Beginners often make the mistake of putting a hard outline around a building, which effectively cuts it off from its surroundings. By contrast, note how Stan Perrott emphasizes light-struck areas with hard edges, while "losing" some edges in the shadows. This emphasizes the advancing and receding planes of the building and renders it more sympathetic with its surroundings.

Delta Farm by Stan Perrott.

◀ ◀ ◀ Strong tonal contrasts between the building and background make for a more powerful image. Hard edges give crispness and definition in the light-struck areas.

◀ ◀ Cast shadows emphasize forms.

◀ Lost edges give a sense of atmosphere. Subtle gradations of color prevent large areas from looking flat and monotonous.

CHAPTER SIX •

Skies

INTRODUCTION

It may seem odd to devote a whole section to skies — they are, after all, an integral part of landscape — but from the painter's point of view, they are a major subject in themselves. They demand close observation and a degree of technical know-how, partly because of their infinite variety and partly because they are not subject to the same rules that govern the solid earth below. A mountain, cliff, or tree will change in appearance under different lighting conditions, but its structure will remain stable, whereas clouds, seemingly solid but in fact composed of nothing but air and moisture, are constantly on the move, forming and re-forming in ways that can only partially be predicted and are never the same twice. Most important of all, the sky is the light source without which the landscape could not exist, and weather conditions above relate directly to the colors, tones, and prevailing mood of the land below. Thus the surest way to spoil a landscape is by failing to analyze or express this relationship.

Clear skies

We tend to think of cloudless skies as simply blue, but in fact they vary widely according to the season and climate. A midsummer's sky in a hot country will be a warm blue, sometimes tending to violet and often surprisingly dark in tone, whereas a winter sky in a temperate zone is a paler and cooler blue. Nor is a clear sky the same color all over. A frequent mistake is to paint blue skies in one uniform wash, but there are always variations — sometimes slight, but often quite marked. As a general rule, skies are darker and warmer in color at the top and paler and cooler on the horizon, following the same rules of aerial perspective as the land. There is, however, an important exception to this. Sky directly over the sea will absorb particles of moisture, giving a darker band of color at the horizon, and a similar effect can often be seen in cities, where the dark band is caused by smoke, dust, or other pollution.

"Learning" clouds

There are few people, whether they paint or not, who can fail to be enthralled by cloud effects — great dark thunderheads, delicate "mackerel" skies, or the magical effects created by a low evening sun breaking through after a day's rain. Sadly these effects are fleeting, so the landscape painter needs to be in constant readiness to watch, memorize, and sketch.

The British painter John Constable (1776-1837) was fascinated by skies and well understood their leading role in landscape painting. He made endless oil sketches of nothing but skies. Often these were done in a few minutes, but provided him with a storehouse of information that he drew on for his finished paintings. Such quick studies are the ideal means of recording these transient effects: even a rapid pencil sketch of cloud shapes with written notes of the colors will act as an *aide-mémoire* and help you to observe constructively. Photographs are also useful in this context, so long as you use them as part of a learning process and not as models to copy for a painting.

Methods

For novice watercolor painters, skies, particularly those with complex cloud formations, are a daunting subject. You aim at a soft impression and find you have unwanted hard edges, or you try to build up some really dramatic tonal contrast for a stormy sky and overwork the paint, completely ruining the effect. But really clouds are not so very difficult. The trick is to understand the medium well enough to develop your own tricks of the trade. Always be ready to use the element of happy accident. Unintentional backruns and spreading paint may suggest the perfect way of painting rain clouds, while some experiments with the lifting out technique will quickly show you how to paint wind clouds or achieve soft, fluffy white edges without having to go through the more laborious process of reserving highlights. Because of the many problems that skies pose for artists, there are two "troubleshooting" sections in this chapter.

Winter sky by Robert Tilling, RI.

Working on a light stretched paper with a cold-pressed surface, and with his board well tilted, the artist used large brushes to lay very wet washes, later adding further ones wet-on-dry.

Bosham Estuary by Christopher Baker.

The scudding clouds are painted lightly and deftly, with definition restricted to the few lines of crayon that formed the preliminary drawing.

Cloud formations

Clouds are always on the move — gathering, dispersing, forming, and re-forming — but they do not behave in a random way. There are different types of cloud, each with its own individual structure and characteristics.

To paint clouds convincingly you need to recognize the differences. It is also helpful to realize that they form on different levels, and this affects their tones and colors.

Cirrus clouds, high in the sky, are fine and vaporous, forming delicate, feathery plumes where they are blown by the wind. The two types of cloud that form on the lowest level are cumulus clouds, with horizontal bases and cauliflower-like tops, and storm clouds (or thunderclouds) — great, heavy masses that rise up vertically, often resembling mountains or towers. Both these low-level clouds show strong contrasts of light and dark. A storm cloud will sometimes look almost black against a blue sky, and cumulus clouds are extremely bright where the sun strikes them and surprisingly dark on their shadowed undersides.

LIGHT IN THE SKY

The great theatrical effects of light and color in the sky have produced some of the most magnificent and sublime works in the history of art. Glorious sunsets, towering banks of sunlit cumulus cloud, dark, storm-filled skies, the feathery patterns of cirrus cloud against a clear blue expanse: these are the kinds of subject that have attracted artists for generations.

The great landscape artist John Constable declared that "the sky is the source of light in nature and governs everything." Thus, the quality of the light in the sky will have a direct influence on the atmosphere and mood in your landscape paintings. Or at least it should. Inexperienced painters sometimes make the mistake of treating sky and land as two completely separate entities, resulting in a disjointed picture with no real feeling of light. Instead, try to bring the sky and the landscape along simultaneously, bringing some of the sky color into the land and vice versa.

It's also important to compare the tonal relationship between the clouds and the sky, and between the sky and the landscape. For example, the tones in the sky are almost always lighter than those in the land. If you see a dark cloud, rimmed with light, this may look at first glance like the contrast between black and white. If you then look at the branches of a tree in dark silhouette in front of that cloud, you will see that the dark of the cloud suddenly appears, in this context, as a middle gray. Through this delicate balancing of tones you can capture the brilliance of the sky without its appearing to be an unnatural, conflicting, and separate entity within your composition. By relying on observation and analysis of this kind you can paint the most extraordinary skies and find that they can be carried off with conviction, even if they appeared utterly improbable at first.

◄ *Sunrise, Nine Springs* by Ronald Jesty.

▲ *Wartime* by Albert Goodwin.

Ronald Jesty has captured one of those beautiful, accidental phenomena that make the sky a constant source of wonder and inspiration. The dark silhouette of the landscape accentuates the brilliance of the sky and focuses our attention upon the wonderful conformity of the clouds.

Albert Goodwin conveys a powerful feeling of perspective and scale in this painting. See what a large expanse of the canvas is devoted to the broad mass of clouds that scud overhead and draw us into the picture.

SELECT AND SIMPLIFY

Very often when painting skies you will be painting from memory, as everything moves and changes so quickly. You must develop a facility for assessing color, tone, volume, and shape quickly and accurately, something that can be achieved only through constant practice. Before you begin painting, spend some time just watching the changing patterns above. Look, too, at the way in which the sun illuminates the clouds. It may seem chaotic at first, but light has a simple logic when you study it more closely. You will notice, for instance, that the sky is usually lighter near the sun and grows increasingly darker as you look away from the sun. On a clear day the sky directly above is a brilliant blue, which grows lighter and cooler toward the horizon. This color change is noticeable even if the sky is cluttered with clouds. Remember, too, that aerial perspective acts on clouds just as it does on land; white clouds directly above will contrast more strongly with the darker tone of the sky than similar clouds do in the distance.

Clouds are rounded forms, so model them as you would any spherical shape. There will be one main highlight, reflecting light from the sun, while the bottom and sides will reflect color and light from adjacent clouds, the sky, and the earth below. Give the clouds roundness and atmosphere by blending and softening most of their edges wet-in-wet, or by scumbling with thin, dry color.

Be bold

As your painting develops you may be tempted to capture every change and nuance in the sky by repainting again and again. Overworking soon kills the translucence of the sky, however, so resolve to be bold and direct in your execution. Notice how, in many great paintings of skies, the artist has used much freer, broader brushstrokes toward the top of the picture, giving the sky a strong sense of perspective.

In watercolor there is a risk of spoiling a successful landscape painting by adding the sky in afterward. If your courage fails, you might opt for a non-committal sky which, while it won't ruin the picture, certainly won't enhance it. It is better to introduce the sky at an early stage so that the tonal relationships can be built up together. When practicing painting skies in watercolor, make large numbers of quick studies, and be prepared to discard readily anything that goes wrong. Do not be afraid of making mistakes — even the most experienced artists may err — but profit by them and apply what you have learned to the next painting. Refer also to your knowledge of clouds and the characteristics of the different types, particularly how they behave in various kinds of light.

The sky is a constant source of wonder and inspiration. The more you observe it with a painter's eye, the more you will understand its logic, and the greater will be your success in translating these observations onto canvas or paper.

Out of Oban by Ronald Jesty, R.B.A.

This dramatic cloud study was painted in the studio from a pen sketch. Although it was built up entirely by means of superimposed washes painted wet-on-dry, the colors are nevertheless fresh and clear. Although many watercolorists avoid overlaying washes for subjects such as these, which are easily spoiled by too great a build-up of paint. Jesty succeeds because he takes care to make his first washes as positive as possible. Notice the granulated paint in the clouds, caused by laying a wet wash over a previous dry one, an effect often used to add extra surface interest.

Moonlit Mackerel Sky, France by William Lionel Wyllie.

By making numerous, quick studies of skies, like this one by William Lionel Wyllie, you will develop your powers of observation and analysis, as well as the technical skill required to describe the effects of light in the sky.

Creating drama

Painting skies effectively requires a combination of boldness and good planning. Know what colors you're going to use at the outset and have them mixed ready so you can work quickly and directly. Having to break off in the middle of a sweeping wash to mix up more paint is likely to prove fatal.

Don't be afraid to mix much stronger, richer pigments than you think you'll need. The color may look too strong when it's wet, but you'll be amazed at how much paler it appears when the wash has dried. Also, don't forget that the dark tones in the landscape will "knock back" the paler tone of the sky even more.

Boldness also means using large brushes, well loaded with paint, and working quickly and loosely so as to inject a sense of movement into the sky. Be spontaneous: there's no point in trying to paint the sky exactly as you see it, since the shapes change so quickly, and if you try to "fix" them you end up with "concrete" clouds.

To create balance in a landscape painting, either the land *or* the sky must dominate. If you choose the latter, make sure that it is composed well and contains a strong center of interest.

TROUBLESHOOTING

The laws of perspective apply to the sky just as they do to the land — yet so many perfectly good landscape paintings are ruined by a sky that looks like a limp curtain hanging at the back of the scene. In the painting on the right, for example, the sky appears curriously vertical. The clouds are too similar in size and shape, and they're too evenly spaced, destroying the illusion of the sky receding into the distance. In addition, the patches of blue sky are too uniform in tone and color, without any gradations to indicate atmospheric perspective.

Another mistake here is in placing the horizon line too high up, so that the land competes with the sky for attention. If you want the sky to be the main feature, lower the horizon line so that the land becomes subordinate.

In contrast to the problem painting, *Somerset Levels* by Lucy Willis (opposite), gives an exciting impression of the vastness of the sky. The way the picture is composed, with a very low horizon line, makes us feel involved in the scene, as if we were actually standing in the field looking up at the heaped clouds advancing toward us. Note also how the clouds overlap each other, creating an interesting diversity of shape and design.

Linear perspective

Clouds appear smaller, flatter and closer together as they recede into the distance, often merging into a haze at the far horizon. Perspective can be heightened even further in your painting by making the nearest clouds much larger, taller, and more clearly defined than the others, as Lucy Willis has done in *Somerset Levels.*

Atmospheric perspective

In creating a sense of perspective in the sky, it helps to think of it as a vast dome stretched over the landscape, rather than a mere backdrop to it. Creating this dome-like impression means applying the laws of

A sense of depth is important when painting skies.

atmospheric perspective as well as linear perspective.

The sky directly overhead is clearer than at the horizon because we see it through less atmosphere. As we look into the distance, intervening particles of dust and water vapor in the air cast a thin veil over the landscape and sky, making them appear grayer and less distinct.

Reproducing the effects of aerial perspective in your sky paintings will greatly increase the impression of depth and atmosphere. In *Somerset Levels*, the "white" clouds near the horizon are tinged with blue-gray, whereas those in the foreground are brighter and clearer. Accentuate the effect of atmospheric haze by blurring the edges of the farthest clouds wet-in-wet and reserving any crisp edges for those in the foreground. It all comes down to close observation and developing the technique to show what you see.

Somerset Levels by Lucy Willis.

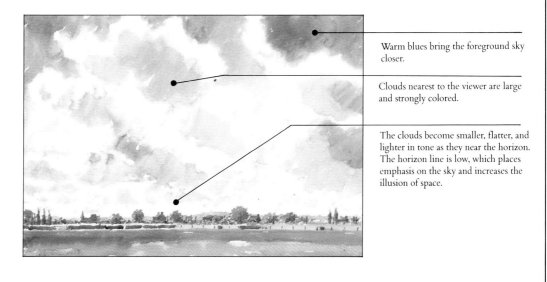

Warm blues bring the foreground sky closer.

Clouds nearest to the viewer are large and strongly colored.

The clouds become smaller, flatter, and lighter in tone as they near the horizon. The horizon line is low, which places emphasis on the sky and increases the illusion of space.

TROUBLESHOOTING

When painting clouds, the chief fault is nearly always timidity, while overworking runs a close second. Timidity results in little, shapeless, "cotton puff" clouds, usually created by dabbing gingerly at the wet sky wash with a piece of tissue to lift out pale shapes — as is the case in the painting on the right. It needs to be emphasized that clouds actually have form; they're not just reversed-out shapes. On the other hand, pushing the paint around and generally overworking the colors tends to result in clouds that look as heavy as lumps of concrete.

The colors and shapes of clouds can change very quickly, and this often causes the novice painter to panic and make a mess of things. The solution lies in learning to harness the light, fluid qualities of watercolor and working quickly and spontaneously to capture a fleeting impression of clouds instead of trying to create a photographic copy.

In *Mountain Retreat* by Moira Clinch (opposite) the clouds are painted very simply, yet they have three-dimensional form as well as radiating light and luminosity.

Keep it fresh

Resist the temptation to push the paint around too much when you're painting clouds, as this quickly destroys the freshness and translucence that is so vital in a sky painting. Decide which colors you want to use *before* you start painting — don't muddle them around on the paper trying to get them "just right." To retain maximum transparency, keep your color mixes simple: why mix three pigments when one or two will do the job far better?

Good timing

Apply your colors with as few brushstrokes as possible. The more you push and prod, the less cloud-like your clouds will become. If you do need to modify an area, remember that correct timing is vital. If you

Making clouds look realistic is a challenge for any painter.

apply a second wash while the first is still wet, or when it has dried too much, there's a danger of unsightly streaks and marks. The second the shine begins to go off the first wash is generally the optimum time to add a second wash.

Three dimensions

Most clouds, particularly heaped cumulus clouds, are three-dimensional and have distinct planes of light and shadow. In *Mountain Retreat* Moira Clinch uses a variety of warm and cool grays to model the shadowed parts of the clouds, leaving small areas of bare white paper to stand for the sunlit highlights.

Pay attention to the edges of the clouds, too. Clouds are predominantly soft-edged, although cumulus clouds also have some hard edges, particularly where the lightest part of the cloud is outlined against a deep blue sky.

Mountain Retreat by Moira Clinch.

Here the artist uses a clean, damp brush to make scumbled strokes at the edges of the clouds to give a soft, vaporous effect.

Cloud shadows are modeled with warm and cool grays built up from light to dark. Slivers of bare paper create bright highlights in backlit clouds.

A variety of hard and soft edges gives form to the clouds. Color is scumbled and lifted out to give movement and a vaporous effect.

CHAPTER SEVEN

Still Life and Animals

INTRODUCTION

There was a time when drawing objects such as plaster casts, bottles, and bowls of fruit was regarded as the first step in the training of art students. Only after a year or two spent perfecting their drawing technique would they be allowed to move on to using paint, while the really "difficult" subjects such as the human figure were reserved for the final year. This now seems an arid approach, almost designed to stifle any personal ideas and talent, but like many of the teaching methods of the past it contained a grain or two of sense — drawing and painting "captive" subjects is undeniably a valuable exercise in learning to understand form and manipulate paint. But still-life painting can be very much more than this. It is enormously enjoyable, and presents almost unlimited possibilities for experimenting with shapes, colors, and composition as well as technique.

The great beauty of still life lies in its controllability. You, as artist, are entirely in charge: you decide which objects you want to paint, arrange a set-up that shows them off to advantage, and orchestrate the color scheme, lighting, and background. Best of all, particularly for those who dislike being rushed, you can take more or less as long as you like over the painting. If you choose fruit and vegetables, they will, of course, shrivel or rot in time, but at least they will not move. This degree of choice allows you to express your own ideas in an individual manner, whereas in a portrait or landscape painting you are more tied to a specific subject.

The still-life tradition

Almost all artists have at some time turned their hands to still life, and long before it became an art form in its own right, lovely little still lifes often appeared among the incidental detail in portraits and religious paintings. The first pure still-life paintings were those with an allegorical significance which became popular in the sixteenth century. Typical of these paintings, known as *vanitas*, were subjects such as flowers set beside a skull, signifying the inevitable triumph of death. It was the Flemish and Dutch painters of the seventeenth and eighteenth centuries, though, who really put still-life and flower painting on the map, with their marvelously lavish arrangements of exotic fruit and flowers, rich fabrics, and fine china and glass. The *vanitas* still lifes reminded their religious patrons of the transience of life, but these exuberant and unashamedly materialistic works, painted for the wealthy merchant classes, were celebrations of its pleasures.

Still-life painting has remained popular with artists ever since, and although it was regarded as an inferior art form by the French Academy, who favored painting with grand historical or mythological themes, it gained respectability when the Impressionists altered the course of painting forever. The still-life paintings of Edouard Manet (1832-83), Paul Cézanne (1839-1906), and Vincent van Gogh (1853-90) rank among the finest works of any kind ever produced, the everyday subject matter being transcended in such a way that paintings become personal and passionate artistic statements.

We will begin with still-life techniques, moving on to animals.

Still Life with Pheasant and Hyacinth by Cherryl Fountain.

This artist also paints landscapes, in the same highly detailed style, but she likes still life particularly because she can control her set-up in a way that allows her to express her love of pattern and texture.

FRUIT AND VEGETABLES

Fruits and vegetables are always popular in still life arrangements. Not only do they have fascinating surface textures, but their colors and shapes can be all-important in lending balance to the composition. For example, a painting that is light in tone overall can be given just the right amount of contrast by the addition of a bunch of black grapes; alternatively, dramatic chiaroscuro effects can be achieved by introducing pale, luminous green grapes or pieces of lemon into a dark painting.

As with flowers, fruits and vegetables look best when they are not forced into a rigid arrangement. Try to place them so that they appear to have just spilled out of a basket, and introduce variety by including pieces of cut fruit or vegetables such as onions and cabbages, chopped in half to reveal their inner patterns.

Beginners often make the mistake of rendering shadows by adding black to make a darker version of the local color of the object. In fact, colors become cooler as they turn into shadow, and contain elements of their complementary color. For example, the shadow side of an orange will contain a hint of its complementary color, blue. In addition, shadows often contain subtle nuances of reflected light picked up from nearby objects.

Highlights, too, are worth close scrutiny. Even the brightest highlight on a shiny apple is rarely pure white. If the prevailing light is cool, the highlight might contain a hint of blue; if the light is warm, the highlight may have a faint tinge of yellow. By paying attention to such details, you will give your paintings a feeling of light and form.

Apples

Here is another simple watercolor study, in which the artist uses transparent washes and glazes to model the form of the apples and bring out their luscious texture.

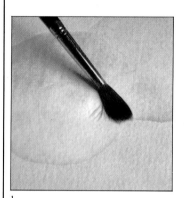

1 With a mixture of sap green and cadmium yellow, the artist blocks in the overall shapes of the apples on damp paper. This is allowed to dry before moving on to the next stage.

2 Working wet-in-wet, the artist brushes in mixtures of sap green and brown madder alizarin to build up form and color, leaving small areas of the pale underwash to create highlights.

3 The reds and greens are strengthened further with transparent glazes, and the artist follows the contours of the apples with his brushstrokes. In places the color dries with a hard edge. This gives the impression of the crisply modeled form of an apple, which differs from the smooth roundness of an orange or a peach. When the apples are complete, the stalks are painted with raw sienna and a touch of ultramarine.

Finally, the cast shadows of the apples are painted with washes and glazes of indigo and purple madder alizarin. A clean, damp brush is used to soften the shadows so that they don't look to harsh. This also gives an impression that the apples are sitting on a shiny surface.

Still Life with Apples by Shirley Felts.

For this lovely painting, delicate but strong, the artist has chosen a plain brown background that picks up the color of the tabletop. But she has not painted it flat: there are several different colours and tones in the "brown," including a deep blue, and she has given movement and drama to it by the use of brushstrokes that follow the direction of the spiky leaves. She builds up her rich colors and softly modeled forms gradually by laying wash over wash, but avoids tired and muddy paint by repeated soaking of the paper. Highlights are lifted out while the paper is wet, and the shadows are deepened later.

Backgrounds

One of the commonest mistakes in still-life painting is to treat the background as unimportant. It is easy to feel that only the objects really matter and that the spaces behind and between them are areas that just need to be filled in somehow. All the elements in a painting should work together, however, and backgrounds, although they may play a secondary role, require as much consideration as the placing of the objects.

The kind of background you choose for an arranged group will depend entirely on the kind of picture you plan. A plain white or off-white wall could provide a good foil for a group of elegantly shaped objects, such as glass bottles or tall vases, because the dominant theme in this case would be shape rather than color, but a group you have chosen because it allows you to exploit color and pattern would be better served by a bright background, perhaps with some pattern itself.

The most important thing to remember is that the background color or colors must be in tune with the overall color key of the painting. You can stress the relationship of foreground to background when you begin to paint, tying the two areas of the picture together by repeating colors from one to another. For example, if your group has a predominance of browns and blues, try to introduce one of these colors into the background also. It is usually better in any case not to paint it completely flat.

STILL LIFE WITH FRUIT

The artist has used a number of different techniques to give a lively look to this bright fruit and vegetable group. His approach was unusual too, since he began by painting in the basic colors of the fruit, leaving the background and the table unpainted until a relatively late stage. This artist frequently paints piece by piece in this way, instead of adopting the more usual method of working all over the painting at the same time. It can be very successful, as it is here, but it does rely on the ability to judge tones and colors very accurately and upon having a clear idea of how the painting is to look finally.

A watercolor containing small, intricate shapes like these requires some planning, as too much overpainting and overlapping of colors can result in a muddy, tired-looking painting in which the brilliance of the colors is lost or diminished. In this case, the artist has solved the problem by using the watercolor mixed with white gouache, which gives it extra covering power without dulling the colors.

Once the colors of the fruit had been established, the warm ochre of the table top was laid on. The paint was applied around the shapes of the fruit, but quite boldly and loosely without too much concern about occasional overlapping. Texture was given to the wood by spattering opaque paint from a stiff brush and then by dragging the same brush, used rather dry, along the surface to suggest wood grain. The fruit was worked up and given more color and form, and then the near-black background was painted in, giving an even richer glow to the fruit and providing a diagonal which balances the composition and brings all the elements in the painting together.

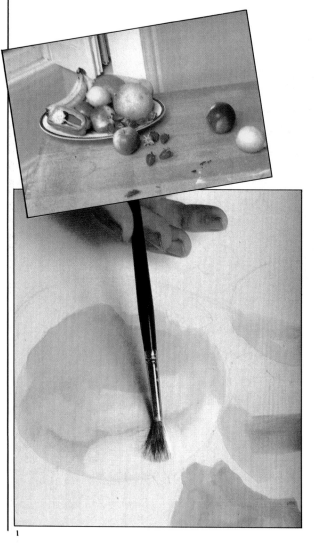

2

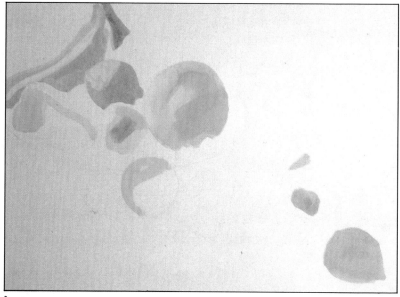

1

1 The artist begins by painting the lemons, using watercolor mixes with just a little white gouache.

2 By painting all the yellow areas first the artist has to a large extent established the composition. The pattern formed by the yellow shapes, interspersed with darker or more vivid forms and colors, is an important element in the painting.

3 Here the artist is working wet-into-wet to build up the forms and colors. Because he is using semi-opaque paint, he is able to lay a lighter yellow on top of the deep orange.

4 Now all the colors of the fruit have been laid on, although not in their final form. This enables the artist to gauge the color and tone for the table top.

5

6

3

7

4

5 Having laid on the basic color for the table top, taking it around the edges of the fruit, the artist now uses the spatter method to give a slight textural interest.

6 The grain of the wood is suggested by dragging a stiff, broad brush over the surface, using a darker color in a slightly dry mixture.

7 This detail show how well the solidity of the fruit has been depicted, being built up with quite broad and bold areas of color. The dark shadows beneath them anchor them to the horizontal plane of the table.

8

8 The addition of the black background gives a further sparkle to the clear, bright colors of the fruit. The textured highlights on the top of the orange were made by dribbling wet, opaque white paint from the brush on top of the darker color.

9 The finished painting shows how important the greatly angled diagonal formed by the back edge of the table is to the composition. It balances the opposing diagonal formed by the group of fruit itself, a triangle with the bowl as the apex.

9

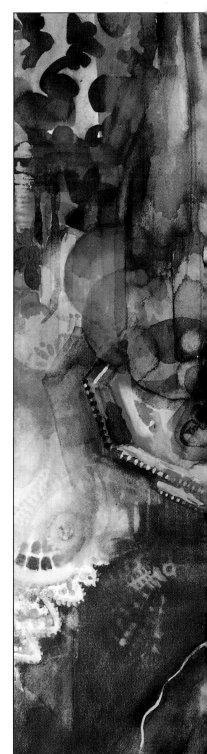

Arranging the group

Planning the disposition of objects in a still-life group so that they provide a satisfactory balance of shapes and colors is as important as painting it, so never rush at this stage, and think carefully about the composition.

A good still life, like any other painting, should have movement and dynamism, so that your eye is drawn into the picture and led around it from one object to another. It is wise to avoid the parallel horizontals formed by the back and front of a table-top, since the eye naturally travels along straight lines and these will lead out of the painting instead of into it. A device often used to break up such horizontals is to arrange a piece of drapery so that it hangs over the front of the table and forms a rhythmic curve around the objects. An alternative is to place the table at an angle so that it provides diagonal lines that will lead inward to the center of the picture.

Never arrange all the objects in a regimented row with equal spaces between them, as this will look static and uninteresting. Try to relate them to one another in pictorial terms by letting some overlap others, and give a sense of depth to the painting by placing them on different spatial planes, with some near the front of the table and other toward the back. Finally, make sure that the spaces between objects form pleasing shapes — these "negative shapes" are often overlooked, but they play an important part in composition.

Black Grapes and Wine by Shirley Trevena.

Trevena works straight from her arranged group, with no sketching or preliminary pencil drawing, and composes as she paints, constantly improving on her group to create balance, harmony, and contrast. She likes to vary the texture of her paint, using thin watercolor washes in places and thickly built-up layers of gouache in others. The lace is the original white paper left untouched. Her work has a lyrical, semi-abstract quality: the objects are all recognizable, but we are drawn to the painting by the shapes and colors.

CREATING PATTERNS

The structure of this painting depends upon the development of negative shapes — that is, the spaces between the objects rather than the objects themselves. The image is built up as a jigsaw pattern of small patches of color which are brought together in the final stages of the painting. This is a useful approach in any medium; however, with watercolor, you must be precise from the start, as it is too transparent to be heavily corrected.

The painting is small and loosely described, and thus you will not need a large range of brushes or colors. Lay in broad washes of color with a loaded brush, letting the bristles spread; draw the hairs to a fine point to describe small shapes and linear details. The whole painting should be allowed to dry frequently, so that the layers of color stay clear and separate, building up gradually to their full intensity. Balance the contrast of warm and cool tones with the hot reds and yellows of the chairs standing out from the cooler green and blue background.

Dark patches of color can be lightened by gently rubbing over them with a clean, wet cotton swab, but try to keep corrections to a minimum or the surface may be damaged. When the image is completely dry, work over the shapes with colored pencils. This modifies the colors and adds a grainy texture to the flat washes.

1

2

3

4

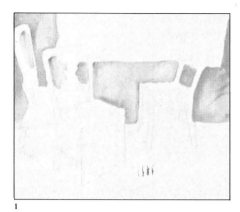

5

1 Very lightly draw the shapes with an HB pencil. Work into the background with washes of burnt sienna, Prussian blue, yellow ochre, and violet with a No. 6 brush.

2 Move across the painting laying in patches of thin color. Add emerald green and viridian to the range of colors.

3 Develop color contrasts by working into the shape of the chairs with yellow, red, and orange and intensifying the blue and green of the background.

4 Give the shadows on the chairs and floor depth with touches of blue and violet.

5 Draw into the shapes with the tip of the No. 3 brush to clarify linear structure. Darken the background to heighten the outline of the chairs.

Describing shapes

Here the chair shapes are created by the artist by describing the space around the shapes and leaving the paper bare to describe the chairs. After the painting is thoroughly dry, colored pencils are used to strengthen shadows and color tones. Do not press too hard, for the paper will be fragile due to the paint layer.

USING SHAPES

The freshness of watercolor depends upon the gradual building up from light to dark, and any attempt to create highlights or pale tones in the final stages of the painting will alter the entire character of the medium. Accuracy is thus all-important in the initial structuring of the composition. White shapes must be precise and clean, created "negatively" by careful drawing of surrounding color areas.

A light pencil sketch will help to establish the correct proportions, but complex shapes are outlined directly with a fine sable brush. Block in solid colours quickly, or a hard line will appear around the edges of the shapes. Use large brushes to work into the foreground and background, and lightly spatter paint dripped from the end of a large brush to create a mottled texture.

A limited range of color was used, mixing in black to create dark tones and varying grays with small touches of red and blue. Dry the painting frequently so that colors remain separate and the full range of tone and texture emerges through overlaid washes.

1

2

3

4

5

6

Negative shapes and spattering

A good example of the use of negative shapes. Here the artist creates the white lines in the jacket by describing the red areas around them, rather than by painting the lines.

Spattering to create texture. Using a decorator's brush, the artist holds the brush above the paper and taps its lightly to create a tonal effect.

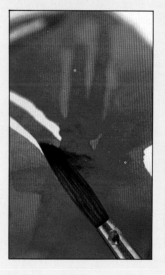

1 Draw the basic shapes of the objects in outline with a pencil. Mix a very thin wash of Payne's gray, and block in the whole of the background.

2 Paint in the local colors of the objects building up the paint in thin layers and leaving white space to show highlights and small details. Keep each color separate.

3 Mix a light brown from red and black, and work over the red, showing folds and creases in the fabric and dark shadows. Lay a wash of brown across the foreground.

4 Work up shadows in the blue in the same way, using a mixture of blue and black. Move over the whole painting putting in dark tones.

5 Strengthen all the colors, breaking up the shapes into small tonal areas. Bring out textural details by overlaying washes and spattering the paint lightly.

6 Intensify the dark brown in the foreground, and use the same brown to indicate shadow on the wall behind. Vary the strength of the color.

TROUBLESHOOTING

When faced with a group of objects for a still-life painting, it's all too easy to choose and arrange them in a way that's haphazard and lacking in thought. The problem is that we tend to choose objects that take our fancy, without stopping to think whether the objects will work together as a group in terms of size, shape, color, and so on. In the still life on the night, for example, we have a wine bottle (the obligatory wine bottle!), a vase of flowers, a hat and a dish towel: two tall, thin shapes and two flat shapes, with nothing to link them together. The student, in common with many beginners, seems averse to the idea of overlapping objects; everything is standing in line, and so the group looks staid and static.

Another common mistake in the design of a still life is to leave too much space around the group. In this painting the objects are lost in a sea of monotonous background.

It is important to compose a still life so that each individual element contributes to the total design. There is a pleasing harmony and rhythm to the objects in Pamela Kay's still-life painting *Tureen of Mandarins with Orange Preserves* (▶). Somehow, everything just "sits right." The group forms a roughly oval shape within the borders of the picture, and everything in the group is organized so as to carry the eye of the viewer on a visual "tour" of the painting. Another nice touch is that each of the objects in the group shares a common theme: they are all kitchen objects, and all are connected with the process of making preserves.

Unify the subject

When you have a group of objects of different size, shape, and color, it is vital that they relate to one another and that the spaces *between* the objects also make interesting shapes. Play around with the arrangement of the objects before starting to paint, and make rough sketches so you can see how the overall shape of the group will look on the paper. Look for points where objects can overlap, because this ties the objects together and creates interesting shape relationships.

This still life does not form a strong image and is rather uninspiring.

Repetition and variation

Try to repeat the shapes and colors within the group, because this sets up visual rhythms which the viewer will respond to. Repeating shapes and forms can also unite and integrate the objects in your still life and prevent them from appearing too scattered.

A word of caution, however: beware of making these repetitions too regular, as this can lead to monotony. Introduce subtle variations of size, shape, or tone to add spice to the design.

In Pamela Kay's painting the rounded shapes of the bowls, the oranges, and the preserve jar create intriguing visual echoes, yet none is exactly like the other. The same applies with the geometric shapes of the other objects. The colors, too, are nicely tied together, with variations on the blue/orange theme repeated throughout.

Tureen of Mandarins with Orange Preserves by Pamela Kay.

Complementary colors — blue and orange — are repeated throughout, creating a lively yet harmonious color scheme.

The repetition of curved and linear shapes gives unity to the group.

The single mandarin pulls the eye down from the fruit bowl, from where it is carried to the left and upward, back to the fruit bowl.

ANIMALS

The animal kingdom presents the commonest of all problems to the would-be recorder of its glories: none of its members stay still long enough to be painted. One can usually bribe a friend to sit reasonably still for a portrait, but you cannot expect the same cooperation from a dog, cat, or horse. If movement is the essence of a subject, however, why not learn to make a virtue of it?

Observing movement

Watch an animal carefully and you will notice that the movements it makes, although they may be rapid, are not random — they have certain patterns. If you train yourself to make quick sketches whenever possible and take photographs as an aid to understanding, you will find that painting a moving animal is far from impossible — and it is also deeply rewarding.

We in the twentieth century are lucky, because we benefit from the studies and observations of past generations. We know, for example, that a horse moves its legs in a certain way in each of its four paces — walking, trotting, cantering, and galloping — but when Edgar Degas (1834–1917) began to paint his marvelous racing scenes he did not fully understand these movements. He painted horses galloping with all four legs outstretched, as they had appeared in English sporting prints. It was only when Eadweard Muybridge (1830–1904) published his series of photographs of animals in motion in 1888 that Degas saw his error and was quick to incorporate the new-found knowledge into his paintings. This points up the value of the camera as a source of reference, but photographs should never be slavishly copied, for this will result in a static, unconvincing image — photographs have a tendency to flatten and distort form and "freeze" movement.

Understanding the basics

Painters and illustrators who specialize in natural history gain their knowledge in a wide variety of ways. Many take powerful binoculars and cameras into remote parts of the countryside to watch and record birds and animals in their natural habitats, but they also rely on illustrations and photographs in books and magazines or study stuffed creatures in museums.

All this research helps them to understand basic structures, such as the way a bird's wing and tail feathers lie or how a horse's or cow's legs are jointed. In the past, artists were taught that a detailed study of anatomy was necessary before they could even begin to draw or paint any living creature. Some wildlife painters, whose prime concern is scientific accuracy, still do this, but for most of us this depth of study is unnecessary.

Sketching from life

Although background knowledge is helpful, because it will enable you to paint with more confidence, books and magazines are never a substitute for direct observation. When you are working outdoors, whether in a zoo or on a farm, try to keep your sketches simple, concentrating on the main lines and shapes without worrying about details such as texture and coloring. If the animal moves while you are in mid-sketch, leave it and start another one — several small drawings on the same page can provide a surprising amount of information.

You may find it difficult at first, but quick sketches are a knack, and you really will get better with practice, partly because you will be unconsciously teaching yourself to really look at your subject in an analytical and selective way. You will also enjoy the freedom sketching allows and the feeling of boldness it generates.

Macaws by Laura Wade.

The artist has made good use of mixed media to build up the birds' vivid colors and delicate textures. Like many professional illustrators, she used photographs as well as drawings from life for her reference; this is the original of a printed illustration in a guide brochure.

PHEASANT

This painting is both a bird study and still-life, since it was painted indoors, and the subject is a stuffed pheasant borrowed from an antique shop. Artists whose particular interest is wildlife can study and observe nature at second hand as well as directly from life. Natural-history books and museums both offer opportunities for gaining a thorough knowledge about structure and detail.

Because there could be no attempt to make the stuffed bird appear anything other than what it was, the painting presented a different challenge from that of representing a live bird. With a live bird the prime consideration might have been to suggest movement, while the natural background of trees or rocks might have formed part of the composition. Here the artist chose to treat the subject in a very formal way, setting it up as a rather stark still life; but his enthusiasm for the bird itself comes across very strongly in the glowing color and the delicately painted detail.

His technique was quite free and fluid, and he worked quickly, building up the form in the early stages from loose washes and working wet-into-wet in places. The background shows an interesting use of watercolor: with only one color a wide variety of tonal contrasts has been achieved. This gives the painting extra drama and excitement as well as providing a balance to the texture of the pheasant itself.

1 A very hard (F) pencil was used to make a careful outline drawing to establish the forms of the bird as well as its relationship to the background and table-top. Composition is extremely important for this subject, which relies for its impact on the way the main shape is placed. Once he had planned the composition, allowing the tail to go out of the frame so that it appears longer, the artist first laid a pale wash on the body and tail.

2 Once the first wash, a mixture of raw umber and cadmium orange, was dry, a darker one using the same colors was laid on top, after which blue and red were applied to the head and neck.

3 The same red, alizarin crimson, was put on the breast area, and the artist then began to work on the head feathers with a fine brush. He used a mixture of black, viridian, and ultramarine for this, leaving parts of the original blue showing through.

4 Some artists work all over a painting at the same time, but in this painting the bird was completed before the artist turned his attention to the background. Here the feathers are being painted, with the paint kept quite loose and fluid to prevent a cramped, overworked look.

5 This detail shows the richness and variety of both the colors and the brushwork. In the red area a darker tone has been allowed to overlap the one below, creating a series of edges which give the impression of feathers. Note how small lines of white have been left in the original wash to stand for the wing feathers.

6

7

6 The painting of the bird is now complete, and the successive washes built up one over the other have created exactly the rich impression that the artist wanted. When putting washes over other washes in this way it is essential to know when to stop; if the surface of the paper becomes too clogged with paint the painting will begin to look tired. Judging the strength of color needed for each wash takes some practice, since watercolor looks so much darker when it is wet.

7 Now the artist begins to work on the background, using a fairly strong mixture of Payne's gray and taking it very carefully around the bird's body. It is often necessary to turn the board sideways or upside down for this kind of work.

8 By varying the tones of the background wash, the artist has made the bird stand out in a very three-dimensional way. The dark head is prevented from merging into the similar tone behind it by the thin line of white that has been left between the two. The white area of the table-top has been carefully placed so that it is not quite central and thus provides a balance to the long, almost horizontal, line of the tail.

8

Pheasant.

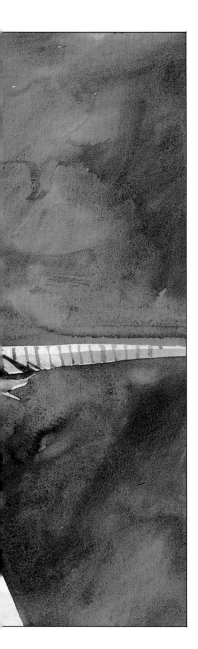

Wild animals

Painting wild creatures in their natural habitats is becoming an increasingly specialized branch of art, mainly because it involves so much more than simply painting. Professional wildlife artists devote their lives to watching and studying birds and animals in the field, often using sophisticated equipment such as powerful binoculars and cameras with telephoto lenses. However, this does not mean that wild animals are beyond the reach of the ordinary artist. Wildlife is the bread and butter of these specialist painters, and their patrons often require a high standard of accuracy, but not all those who want to paint animals need be so constrained.

There is no need, either, to choose inaccessible subjects. Deer, for example, are eminently paintable and will often come quite close to the viewer in country parks, while shyer, more exotic creatures can be studied and sketched at zoos. A zoo, of course, is not a true habitat for a lion, tiger, or monkey, so if you want to use such sketches for a finished painting of a tiger in a forest you may have to resort to books and magazines for a suitable setting. There is nothing wrong with this — after all, not everyone has the opportunity to paint the forests of Asia and Africa from first-hand experience.

Brown Hare by John Wilder.

It may seem surprising that this lovely, delicate painting was done in gouache, but it provides an excellent demonstration of the versatility of the medium. Although usually associated with bright, bold work, it can be used as effectively for thin, pastel-colored washes as for vivid, rich impastos. One of its problems is that it dries out very quickly on the palette, but Wilder solves this by using a version of the special palette sold for acrylic, a simple device consisting of wet blotting paper under a layer of greaseproof paper (a British product similar to waxed paper). The paints are laid out on the greaseproof and, if covered between working sessions, will stay moist indefinitely.

He started by transferring the main outlines from a working drawing and then laid several very pale overall base washes before beginning to build up the head and body of the hare. Because he likes to leave the outline vague and the brushwork blurred until the final stages, his working process is one of continual painting, blurring, re-defining, overpainting, and removing excess paint by sponging or scraping.

The grass was painted when the hare was almost complete, beginning with barely colored water and very gradually increasing the strength. The final touch was to wash over the hare once or twice with the background color, to unify the composition and avoid the cardboard cut-out look seen in many less successful animal paintings.

FEATHERS

In most birds, the wing and tail feathers are quite smooth and precise in shape, while those on the neck and throat have a downy quality. Begin by painting the bird with a pale underwash. Then use a small, soft brush to delineate the markings of the main feathers, working wet over dry to achieve a precise pattern. The soft, downy feathers should be added last, using light, scumbled strokes.

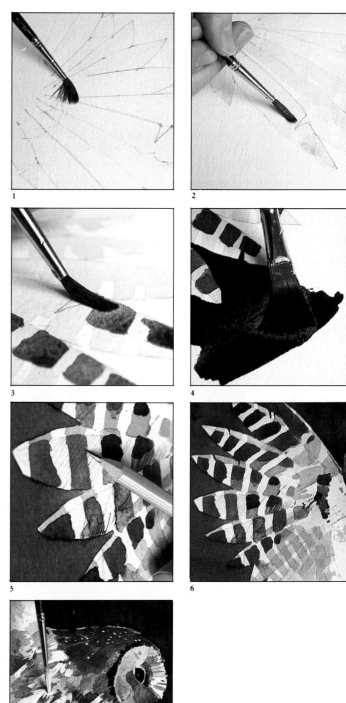

In this dramatic study of an owl in flight, the artist uses very loose brushmarks, which not only capture the texture of the feathers but also accentuate the impression of flight.

For obvious reasons it can be difficult to study birds from life, but working from a photograph is not always satisfactory. In this particular case, a high-quality photograph provided a ready-made composition, but the artist also made studies of a dead owl which he had found, so that he could record the coloring and arrangement of the feathers more accurately.

1 Detail from the wing feathers. The artist begins with a fairly accurate outline drawing of the bird and then blocks in the lightest tones of the wing feathers with a No. 4 sable brush and a very pale wash of yellow ochre.

2 When the first wash is dry the artist begins to indicate the patterning on the feathers with a middle tone of burnt sienna and raw umber.

3 With a dark mixture of burnt sienna and ivory black, the darkest pattern on the feathers is blocked in.

4 The drama of the painting lies in the clear, light shape of the owl against the inky black sky. Here the artist is blocking in the dark background with a very dark wash of Payne's gray. He first cuts carefully around the precise shapes of the feathers using a No. 2 sable brush. Once safely away from the edges of the feathers, he uses a ½in (1.2cm) flat Dalon brush to complete the background.

5 The artist now adds just a hint of texture to some of the feathers by applying hatched lines with a sharp HB pencil.

6 This close-up of the main wing feathers shows how the patterns and shapes have been built up, starting with the latest tones and working up to the darks in the glazing technique. The process is very simple, but highly effective because it is so direct and to the point.

7 The feathers on the neck and the underside of the wing have a quite different quality from that of the sharply defined wing feathers. To indicate their thick, downy texture, the artist first applies various tones of Payne's gray, ivory black, and cadmium yellow with overlapping strokes. When these are dry, white gouache is applied with rapid brushmarks, overlapping the darker feathers in places. This semi-opaque color has the effect of softening the appearance of the feathers. Finally, white gouache is spattered lightly over the top of the head to give the characteristic markings (the rest of the picture was carefully masked off with newspaper to protect it from any stray droplets of paint).

Gouache

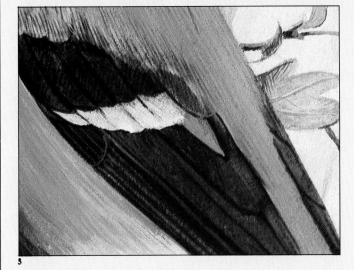

By using gouache, as opposed to watercolor, one can achieve a much greater level of detail. This allows greater precision in the shape of the wing and tail feathers of this finch.

1 Once the washes of base color have have dried, you can start adding details to the plumage, gradually building up the color and texture. The artist here has used a very dry brush with the occasional touch of liquid paint to emphasize the changes in tone, and to bring vitality to the image.

2 The vivid colors of the breast feathers are added in crimson and cadmium red. The texture of the feathers on the back is built up in tones of gray, using a fine sable brush.

3 Stroke by stroke, the artist creates the fine texture of the back feathers. Highlights have been added using white paint, and here he is adding darker tones using a No. 0 sable brush.

4 Using a very small sable brush the artist paints fine, parallel strokes in dry, undiluted paint to add the final touches to the plumage. This hatching technique is particularly good for conveying the texture of feathers.

5 In this detail, you can see the wide range of tones used, and the careful hatching and cross-hatching of the strokes.

EYES

The eyes are often the most expressive feature of an animal or bird, so they are worthy of some attention. In creatures that are natural predators, for example, the eyes have a hard, watchful, imperious quality, which should be emphasized with hard, crisply defined outlines.

Compare this quality to the soft, vulnerable appearance of the eyes of young animals and of non-predatory species such as horses, cows, and deer. Pale colors and a smudgy technique will portray the dewy,

liquid look of these eyes.

The eyes of animals and birds have a pronounced spherical shape and their surface is glassy and highly reflective. Applying your colors in thin glazes is the best way to capture the subtle nuances of light and shade that give the eyes their depth and three-dimensionality. Pay attention also to the shapes of the highlights and shadows, which follow the convex contour of the eyeball.

The transparence of watercolor makes it an excellent medium for rendering the subtle nuances of tone and color that give eyes their unique depth and three-dimensionality.

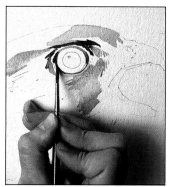

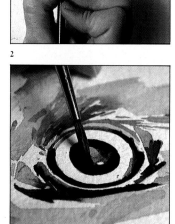

1 Working on a sheet of stretched 200lb Bockingford watercolor paper, the artist sketches a simple outline shape for the eye with an HB pencil.

2 The artist begins by painting the area surrounding the eye with pale washes of Payne's gray and cobalt blue mixed with yellow ochre. Using a No. 2 round sable brush, he then defines the outer rim of the eye with ivory black.

3 The feathers surrounding the eye are built up further with washes of cobalt blue and yellow ochre. Then the pupil of the eye is painted with cobalt blue, leaving a tiny dot of white paper for the brightest highlight.

4 The darks of the pupil are gradually built up with repeated glazes of cobalt blue and Payne's gray. Because each glaze shines up through the next one, the color has a depth that captures the glassiness of the bird's eye. The darkest part of the pupil is painted with ivory black.

5 When the pupil is completely dry the artist paints the iris with a mixture of brown madder alizarin and cadmium orange. This is allowed to dry thoroughly before adding the next wash.

6 The round form of the eye is developed by adding a shadow wash over the iris with a mixture of burnt sienna and cadmium orange. In this close-up, notice how the artist has used a combination of hard and soft edges to define the form of the eye and prevent it from looking too static. The gradual build-up of washes helps to define the convex contour of the eyeball.

7 The clean, sharp, bright highlight of the eagle's eye conveys the fact that this bird is very much a predator.

Movement

When we watch an animal in movement, such as a horse galloping, our eyes take in an overall impression of shape and color but no precise details — these become blurred and generalized in direct ratio to the speed of the animal's movement. The best way of capturing the essence of movement is to choose a technique that in itself suggests it, so try to keep your work free and unfussy, applying the paint fluidly and letting your brush follow the direction of the main lines.

Alternatively, you could try watercolor pastels or crayons, which can provide an exciting combination of linear qualities and washes. A sketchy treatment, perhaps with areas of paper left uncovered, will suggest motion much more vividly than a highly finished one — the surest way to "freeze" a moving animal is to include too much detail. This is exactly what the camera does: a photograph taken at a fast shutter speed gives a false impression because it registers much more than the human eye can. Photographs, though, are enormously useful for helping you to gain an understanding of the way an animal moves, and there is no harm in taking snapshots to use as a "sketchbook" in combination with direct observation.

Dog's eyes
Using a very fine No. 0 sable brush, the artist painted the eyes in layers of the same color, after each previous one had dried, to build up the density of color. The paint was laid on thinly to achieve a soft finish, leaving the paper white for the whites of the eyes.

Tiger's eyes
The expression in this tiger's eyes is bold and unfaltering, accentuated by the small size of the pupils and the hard, glinting highlight.

Chimpanzee's eyes
The eyes of this young chimpanzee — a non-predator — are much softer. There is much more light in the eye, and the outer rim is less sharply defined.

TROUBLESHOOTING

Animals make delightful painting subjects, but unfortunately, they tend not to sit still for long. It can be very frustrating when your "model" suddenly gets bored and wanders off, leaving you with a half-finished painting, and for this reason many people prefer to work from a photograph of their pet. Generally, however, this is not a good idea because photographs tend to flatten form, distort colors, and reduce textural detail. They also "freeze" the pose of the animal, and this often means that the finished painting, too, lacks life and movement. In the painting on the right, for example, the cat appears unnaturally stiff, like a paper cut-out which has been "stuck on" to the picture surface.

Rendering the soft texture of animal fur also presents problems for beginners. In this example, the student has used too many stiff lines and strokes, with the result that the cat's fur more closely resembles a porcupine's quills. This same mistake is often made when painting human hair: the novice painter attempts to render individual hairs, instead of suggesting the bulk of the hair in terms of soft masses.

It may not always be easy, but painting an animal from life will in the end give you better results than copying from photographs. The secret is to choose a time when your pet is completely relaxed — perhaps when it is snoozing after a meal or basking in the sun — and then paint as quickly as possible.

In *Lucy Asleep* (opposite) artist Sally Michel has used the fluid properties of watercolour paint to capture the sleek, sinuous form of the cat and also the soft texture of its fur. While the cat napped, the artist quickly blocked in weak washes of Naples yellow and yellow ochre to establish the curled shape of the body. She then modeled the contours of the head and body with stronger washes, building up the major planes and masses much as sculptor would. The black markings were added next, using light and dark washes in ivory black, well diluted. The finer details were left till last. Since speed is of the

Capturing the soft texture of animal fur is never easy.

essence, this is the most sensible approach to adopt; the main thing is to capture the characteristic shape and gesture of the animal first, because this is what gives character to the "portrait." Then, even if the animal changes position, you can fill in the finer details such as the nose, claws, and whiskers without too much difficulty.

Work wet-in-wet

To capture the smooth, downy appearance of animal fur, use fast, flowing strokes and think in terms of masses rather than lines. Work up gradually from the palest tones to the darkest, allowing each succeeding wash to blend into the previous one just before it dries, so that fuzzy edges form. Finally, draw in just a few of the fine, long hairs using the tip of a very fine brush.

Lucy Asleep by Sally Michel.

This detail shows how the soft texture of the fur is created by brushing in the darker colors while the lighter ones are still damp. If a color is too dark, or spreads too far, it can be gently blotted with a tissue or soaked up with blotting paper.

· CHAPTER EIGHT ·

Water

INTRODUCTION

Water is one of the most appealing and challenging of all subjects. Like the sky, it presents a multitude of different faces — from wild, wind-tossed waves or turbulent waterfalls to the glassy surface of a still pond. Also like the sky, it is elusive and insubstantial.

Observe and simplify

Perhaps more than any other subject, water requires very close observation. The shapes and colors of trees or hills can, to some extent, be re-created from memory, but water has no permanent shape or presence of its own. A completely still lake will present a mirror image of the sky and any prominent land features behind it, but one tiny breeze can remove these images in a matter of seconds, transforming the water surface into a steely gray, solid-looking mass. A fast-running stream seen from a certain distance away may provide a reassuringly simple surface and an even color, but as soon as you sit down beside it, the real paradox of water becomes apparent. It is undeniably there, but at the same time it is transparent, an ethereal presence through which you can clearly see the sand and rocks below.

To paint water successfully it is necessary to simplify what you see, but you cannot hope to distill the essence of a subject until you are familiar with its complexities. All artists know that water is not easily captured in paint. The great Impressionist painter Claude Monet (1840-1926), for whom it amounted almost to an obsession, spent years trying to reconcile its special qualities with those of paint and canvas. J.M.W. Turner (1775-1851) became a popular subject of contemporary cartoons because of his habit of taking his paints and canvas onto boats in the Thames so that he could study the effects of water more fully.

So be prepared to spend time watching water — it is a pleasing enough pastime in itself. If you sit quietly by a river or on the seashore, you will begin to see that the movements of water, like its changing colors, follow certain patterns, as do the movements of the sky. Understanding, for instance, the way the sea swells to become a wave, which then curls over and under before breaking into foam, will enable you to paint it with assurance and freedom.

Painting methods

As soon as you begin to labor the paint, the effect of movement and fluidity will be destroyed. There are several techniques that are particularly suited to the subject, some of which are shown in the examples on the following pages, but, as a general rule, any method that involves much overlaying of paint should be avoided. Broad, flat or broken washes are ideal for still lake or calm sea, and a dry brush dragged across rough white paper is a wonderfully economical means of suggesting lines or patches of wind-ruffled water in the distance. Ripples and reflections can be described in a kind of shorthand by calligraphic brush marks and squiggles, while the wet-in-wet method is marvelous for a soft, diffused impression and beautifully conveys a misty day when all the colors merge together with no hard lines. Everyone has their own way of painting, however, and ultimately the only way to find out the best way of approaching the subject is by trial and error — the latter will at least show you what not to do.

Low Tide Textures by Robert Tilling.

Robert Tilling lives in the Channel Islands, and most of his watercolors are based on what he calls the "edge of the sea." As can be seen in this painting, he is fascinated by the abstract qualities of such seascapes. He usually works in pure watercolor, used in broad, wet washes, but here he has used a collage technique, involving gluing torn (stretched) paper to the working surface and then applying washes on top. Some color was then scraped off with a piece of stiff cardboard, more washes applied, and some gouache lines added as a final stage.

Loch Etive at Taynuilt by Ronald Jesty.

Jesty has set up such a strong contrast of darks and lights that the patch of white water reflected from the bright area of sky seems almost to be illuminated from behind. The combination of deep-toned, hard-edged washes and the slightly granular texture of the paper is particularly striking.

VIEW OF VENICE

In this demonstration, artist John Martin describes his method of painting water simply and with a minimum of fuss. He begins with broad washes of transparent watercolor, then overlays these with mixtures of watercolor and gouache for the highlights and reflections. Although gouache is opaque, Martin finds that its brilliant, light-reflective qualities are perfect for capturing the sparkling quality of the atmosphere surrounding a body of water.

1 "I begin by plotting the main shapes of the composition in pencil. Then, using a soft, round brush, I apply pale underwashes of blue and gray to establish the overall color key of the painting. For the sky I mix up varying proportions of permanent white, cobalt blue, and ultramarine, and apply the color with loose, scumbled strokes that give a sense of movement."

2 "I add further layers of color and continue to build up the main areas and masses. Using a mixture of ultramarine, vermilion, and white, I make a warm gray, which I use to strike in the shapes of the doors and windows. With the same color, I paint the wavering reflections in the water, using the pointed tip of the brush. Then I roughly indicate the shapes of the boats and their reflections, using cadmium yellow, cobalt blue, ultramarine, burnt umber, and viridian."

View of Venice by John Martin, watercolor and gouache.

3 "Having established the cool blues, I now turn my attention to the warm yellows in the foreground. I indicate reflected sunlight on the nearer buildings with mixtures of lemon yellow, alizarin crimson, and white. Then I add thin washes of yellow in the water. When these are dry I strengthen the details of the boats and reflections, using horizontal and vertical strokes of blue, gray, and white."

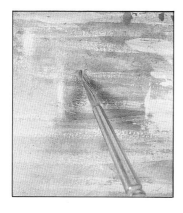

4 "In the final stage I strengthen the darks and touch in the highlights: white on the roofline of the distant buildings, white and lemon yellow on the nearer buildings, and mixtures of white and cobalt blue on the water. In the near foreground I use thicker paint, applied with swift, dry brush strokes, to indicate sparkling light on the water's surface.

"This detail of the water shows how I use a small, just-damp brush and thickish paint to make dry, broken strokes that give a sense of movement and light on the water's surface."

MOVING WATER

A river view that includes a weir or a waterfall offers the artist an opportunity to practice rendering different types of water: the smooth, glassy surface of the calm water upstream, the tumbling white water of the waterfall itself, and the complex ripples and eddies of the water churned up beneath the waterfall. With a subject like this the main pitfall is including too much detail, so that the painting becomes fussy and the fresh, moist feeling is lost: it is essential to

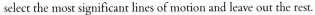

select the most significant lines of motion and leave out the rest.

For this painting of a woodland river, the artist has chosen watercolor as his medium. Watercolor has a unique transparence and freshness which is ideally suited to painting water.

Painting rushing water in watercolor is especially challenging, however, because you can't pile on thick layers of paint to represent churning foam, as you can in oil or acrylics. In this respect, watercolour is an excellent medium with which to practice developing a simple, restrained approach to painting water.

1 Working on a sheet of 200lb Bockingford paper, the artist begins by indicating the dark tones in the water with a pale wash of ultramarine applied with a No. 6 sable brush. The strokes are made smoothly and decisively, leaving areas of white paper for the highlights on the water.

2 At the base of the waterfall, the color is applied thinly in loose, scumbled strokes with the side of the brush to create the effect of churning water.

3 A dark wash of Hooker's green is now brushed in to establish the trees on the bank of the river in the background. Beneath this, a thin strip of white paper is left to indicate a sparkling highlight on the distant water. Then the smooth expanse of water above the waterfall is painted with ultramarine and Hooker's green, mixed wet-in-wet.

4 Using a stiff bristle brush, the artist spatters a pale mixture of ivory black and Hooker's green across the base of the waterfall to give the effect of spray and foam being tossed in the air.

5 Moving toward the foreground now, the artist strengthens the color of the ripples in the water, which reflects some of the dark greens of the foliage overhanging the river bank. The ripples are painted with Payne's gray, Hooker's green, and ultramarine, with the tones becoming progressively lighter toward the foreground.

6 Taking a soft brush moistened with clean water, the artist now softens and blurs the colors in the foreground water to show how the ripples dissipate as they move out from the waterfall. Finally, the background trees are developed with mixtures of sap green. Hooker's green, and ivory black. A little gum arabic is added to stiffen the paint slightly, allowing the artist to push the color around with scumbled strokes. When dry, they leave a delightful impression of dappled sunlight filtering through the trees.

The cool, clear water has been rendered very simply, yet it looks real enough to touch! Notice also how a sense of perspective is retained by making the ripples darker and closer together in the distance.

Scraping back

Sometimes called *sgraffito*, this simply means removing dry paint so that the white paper is revealed. The method is most often used to create the kind of small, fine highlights that cannot be reserved, such as the light catching blades of grass in the foreground of a landscape. It is a more satisfactory method than opaque white applied with a brush, as this tends to look clumsy and, if laid over a dark color, does not cover it very well.

Scraping is done with a sharp knife, such as an X-Acto knife or craft knife, or with a razor blade. For the finest lines, use the point of the knife, but avoid digging it into the paper. A more diffused highlight over a wider area can be made by scraping gently with the side of the knife or with a razor blade, which will remove some of the paint but not all of it.

This technique is not successful unless you use a good-quality, reasonably heavy paper — it should be no lighter than 140lb. On a flimsier paper you could easily make holes or spoil the surface.

The same method can be used for gouache, but only if the surface is one that can withstand this treatment.

The delicate, complex pattern of the frothy water in the painting below was created by scraping with a sharp point. The effect, which can be seen clearly in the detail (◀), would be impossible to achieve by any other means. Opaque white gouache could be used, but the texture would be less interesting and the lines less fine and crisp.

STILL WATER

There are few sights more tempting to the painter than the tranquil, mirror-like surface of a lake on a still day or a calm, unruffled sea at dawn or dusk. But although it would be reasonable to believe still water to be an easy subject, it is surprising how often such paintings go wrong.

The commonest reason for failure is quite simply poor observation. A calm expanse of water is seldom exactly the same color and tone all over, because it is a reflective surface. Even if there are no objects such a boats, rocks, or cliffs to provide clearly defined reflections, the water is still mirroring the sky and will show similar variations. These shifts in color and tone — often very subtle — are also affected by the angle of viewing. Water usually looks darker in the foreground because it is closer to you and thus reflects less light.

It is also important to remember that a lake or area of sea is a horizontal plane. This sounds obvious, but has powerful implications for painting. A horizontal plane painted in an unvaried tone will instantly assume the properties of a vertical one because no recession is implied. It can sometimes be necessary to stress flatness and recession by exaggerating a darker tone or even inventing a ripple or two to bring the foreground forward.

Loch Rannoch. Low Water by Ronald Jesty RBA.

There is not a single unnecessary brushstroke to disturb the calm tranquility of this scene. The artist has cleverly enhanced the bright surface of the water and its pale, sandy banks by setting up strong contrasts of tone while keeping the colors muted. The crisply painted reflections of the dark trees on the right and the little lines of shadow on the left define the river with perfect accuracy. The water surface is not painted completely flat: a sense of space and recession is created by the slightly darker patch of color directly in the foreground, as well as by the linear perspective that narrows the river banks as it flows toward the lake.

The White Cloud. Loch Etive by Ronald Jesty RBA.

It is interesting to compare this painting with the one opposite, by the same artist. The majority of his paintings are in pure watercolor, but here he uses gouache applied in broad areas of very flat color to give an almost print-like effect, in which the juxtaposition of shapes and colors is all-important. He has produced an exciting composition by echoing the sweeping curve of the cloud in the light area of foreground, while the reflections in the water serve to break up the central area of blue-gray.

Noirmont Evening. Jersey by Robert Tilling RL.

The magical effects of still water under a setting sun have been achieved by a skillful use of the wet-in-wet technique. Tilling works on paper with a cold-pressed surface, stretched on large blockboard supports. He mixes paint in considerable quantities in old teacups or small food cans and applies it with large brushes, tilting his board at an angle of 60° or sometimes even more to allow the paint to run. This method, although looking delightfully spontaneous, can easily get out of control, so he watches carefully what happens at every stage, ready to lessen the angle of the board if necessary to halt the flow of the colors. The dark wash for the headland was painted when the first wet-in-wet stage had dried.

TROUBLESHOOTING

Water is one of the most popular painting subjects, yet it isn't an easy one to get right. Reflections, in particular, can be confusing and are often not well understood. Painting reflections in water takes practice and close observation: novice painters usually go wrong because, first, they don't understand the way reflections behave and, second, they are too timid in their approach.

In the painting on the right, the reflections don't ring true because the student hasn't observed them properly. Notice, for example, how the reflections of the angled trees and the boat extend in the same direction: in reality they would lean in the opposite direction, to form a mirror image.

Even the calmest water is often disturbed by ripples and currents that break up and distort reflections, thus creating lovely wavering patterns. But in this painting the reflections are not at all exciting in design; in fact they don't really look like reflections at all! In addition, they are much too pale and wishy-washy, presumably because the artist has assumed that if the water is light in color, reflections, too, must be light.

Fishermen Repairing Nets, Caorle by Ronald Jesty (opposite) is a perfect example of how reflections should be painted. Here, simplicity is the keynote: the reflections of the fisherman and his boat are rendered with dark, limpid washes that give a lifelike impression of the smooth, gently undulating surface of the water.

Techniques
Fluid and transparent, watercolor is tailor-made for painting reflections in water. There are a number of techniques you can use,

Reflections present a devilish challenge to the watercolorist.

depending on the effect you want to convey. In this painting, Ronald Jesty emphasizes the smooth glassiness of the water through the use of strong contrasts of light and dark tone. Transparent glazes are applied one on top of the other to build up a depth of tone and color. (Note how strong and well defined they are, compared to the rather feeble reflections in the problem painting.)

Another interesting technique is to flood the chosen colors onto damp paper and allow them to fuse together wet-in-wet, creating a perfectly still effect.

Fishermen Repairing Nets, Caorle by
Ronald Jesty. Note how the reflection
curves away from the figure.

·INDEX·

Figures in *italics* refer to relevant picture captions.